A Genealogical Dictionary of Wright Families in the Lower Hudson Valley to 1800

Compiled by
Douglas Wright Cruger

HERITAGE BOOKS
2017

HERITAGE BOOKS
AN IMPRINT OF HERITAGE BOOKS, INC.

Books, CDs, and more—Worldwide

For our listing of thousands of titles see our website
at
www.HeritageBooks.com

Published 2017 by
HERITAGE BOOKS, INC.
Publishing Division
5810 Ruatan Street
Berwyn Heights, Md. 20740

Copyright © 1987 Douglas Wright Cruger

All rights reserved. No part of this book may be reproduced or transmitted in any form or by any means, electronic or mechanical, including photocopying, recording or by any information storage and retrieval system without written permission from the author, except for the inclusion of brief quotations in a review.

International Standard Book Numbers
Paperbound: 978-1-55613-090-8

TABLE OF CONTENTS

FORWARD

INTRODUCTION

ABBREVIATIONS

GENEALOGICAL DICTIONARY
OF WRIGHT FAMILIES   1

BIBLIOGRAPHY   143

APPENDIX
Wright Estates Filed After 1800   151

PLACE INDEX   155

NAME INDEX   163

FORWARD

This dictionary began as a search for an illusive Wright ancestor, "lost" in early New York state. The name of Wright is exceedingly common in early America, and a number of early families by the name of Wright have been traced to Long Island and New York's lower Hudson valley. Only a few of the lineages recorded here have proven European connections. Most of them simply appear in the early records, without proven connections beyond the immediate record. Undoubtedly, most of the early New York Wrights came from the British Isles. However, the name of Wright (also Right, Ryte, Ryt) is also found among the early Dutch records, and name is not uncommon in Germany and other countries.

The name of Wright is also common to New England and New Jersey, and it is likely that some of the early New York Wrights have their American origins there. While beyond the scope of this study, some New England Wright families have been included, if their early migration to Long Island and the Hudson Valley has been shown or is suspected. One published source for many New England Wright families, *Genealogical and Biographical Notes of the Descendants of Sir John Wright of Kelvedon Hall, Essex, England, Thomas Wright of Wethersfield, Conn., and Dea. Samuel Wright of Northampton, Mass.* by Curtis Wright (Cambridge MO, 1915), contains records of Wrights who migrated to New York state and west, but well beyond the period under study, and the source has not been used here. Also not included in this study are the many Wright families to be found in early New Jersey Quaker records.

The focus of this study has been Wright migrations to and from Westchester and old Dutchess Counties, then further up the Hudson to Albany County, and west. While a number of Wright families have been located in western New York by 1790, only those families with Hudson Valley origins are included here.

I wish to acknowledge here, with deep gratitude, six men and women who, over a course of years, have helped to collect these records in a search for their "lost" New York Wright ancestors. Much of what follows has come to light as a result of their efforts, and they deserve credit for helping to build the file of early New York Wrights.

Jeanne Bender, Evansville, Indiana
Dorothea White, Los Angeles, California
Mary Kales Witherbee, Oneonta, New York
Joseph V. Wright, Haverford, Penna. (dec'd)
Ray Wright, Wheat Ridge, Colorado (dec'd)
Vincent Wright, Maitland, Florida

                                          Douglas Wright Cruger
                                          Portland, October 1987

INTRODUCTION

Each record stands alone. Given (or Christian) names are listed in alphabetical and rough chronological order. Records are numbered for identification; the numbers do not imply generations or relationship to others of the same given name. Following each given name, the father's given name and identifying number is listed, in brackets, followed by known vital records, probate record, and other information that can be attributed to that individual. Each record ends with the sources for that record only, again in brackets.

Wives of Wrights appear twice in the dictionary, first in bold face type in the husband's record and, second, in their place alphabetically, in lower case letters, with an index reference to their husbands.

Children also appear twice in the dictionary, first in their father's records and, second, either in their own record or else (usually in the case of children born after 1800) in their place alphabetically, with their year of birth (when known) and an index reference to their parent.

The records include abbreviated data only, and, for more detail, the reader is urged to check both the source and whatever primary documents may be available. An annotated bibliography of sources (often abbreviated in the record) is given immediately following the main body of text.

As an additional research tool, an index to probate records filed after 1800 for the counties of Dutchess, Columbia, Greene, Orange, and Albany has been included in an Appendix to the main text. For the most part, material from the probate indexes does not appear in the main body of text.

ABBREVIATIONS

To save print and computer space, abbreviations have been used extensively. States have been abbreviated using the US Postal Code. Other abbreviations commonly used are listed below.

adm Administration
aka also known as
b birth
bro brother
bur buried
bp baptized/christened
ca *circa*, about
Cem Cemetery
Co County
dau daughter
d death
div divorced
est estate
exec executor
husb husband
gf grandfather
IGI International Genealogical Index (Mormon) Microfiche, April 1984
LI Long Island
liv living
m marriage
mortg mortgage
PR Probate Record (ie Surrogate's Court)
perh perhaps (statement without proof)
prob probably (statement by circumstantial evidence)
rec record, recorded

RECORD *New York Genealogical & Biographical Record*. Quarterly.
REGISTER *New England Historical & Genealogical Register*. Quarterly.
say educated guess, within known parameters
sis sister
TAG *The American Genealogist*. Quarterly
Transcript *Genealogical Column of the Boston Evening Transcript*
wf wife

A GENEALOGICAL DICTIONARY OF WRIGHT FAMILIES IN THE LOWER HUDSON VALLEY

A

Aaltje (Marlings) wf [Henry 2]

AARON 1 [John 16]. No further record. [DUTCHESS COUNTY HIST, 498]

ABEL 1 d Coxsackie, Greene Co NY, 28 Dec 1837, m **Eunice---**, and left issue (per will): Hiram (of Coxsackie), Horatio Nelson (of Rochester NY), Ophelia m James Turner, Albert H (of NYC), Adaline, Eliza Ann, Olney F (of Coxsackie), Maria (dec'd) m William Redding, Aurelia m Wm H Clark. [GreCoNY PR 480-10639, D:166]

ABIGAIL 1 [John 5] b Oyster Bay LI 17 Jan 1712/3 m **John Feake** b ca 1707 d 8 Mar 1749/50 ae 43. ["Early Ludlam...Families", in TAG 14:8; "The Feake Family," by George E McCracken in RECORD 87:109]

ABIGAIL 2 m (License) 16 Jul 1762 **Robert Rosseter**. [WRIGHT MARR, 49]

ABIGAIL 3 [Daniel 16] m **Adolphus Latting** b 20 May 1768 d Michigan 21 Sep 1840 son Benjamin & Deborah (Holmes) Latting. Res Monkton, Addison Co VT. ["The Latting Family" by John J Latting, in RECORD (1871), 2:54; WRIGHT/OB by Perrine]

ABIGAIL 4 [Samuel 10] b 2 Dec 1781 m **Godfrey**

Radner, and had issue (bp Bethlehem RDC Berne NY): Jacob 1801, Peggy 1802. [BETHLEHEM RECORDS by Christoph, p 19]

ABIGAIL 5 [Adam 3]

ABIGAIL 6 [Jacob 1]

Abigail (---) wf [John 19]
Abigail (Barker) wf [John 5]
Abby (Cunningham) wf [Daniel 23]
Abigail (Goodrich) wf [Cruger 1]
Abigail (Soule) wf [Wise 2]
Abigail (Whittemore) wf [Enos 1]

ABIJAH 1 [Benjamin 1] b prob WestCoNY 13 Nov 1763 m perh ----Hunt (per Frost). [Perrine has it that his sis Elizabeth m ----Hunt] Perh rec Frederickstown DutCoNY 1790. Acct with Dr Cornelius 6 Jun 1791 to 13 Dec 1803 names "girl, wf, son, inf, Joseph, Raynor, 2 chn, Benjamin, Nathaniel." Issue (from father's 1812 will): Sarah, Elizabeth, Benjamin, Joseph, also prob Nathaniel. [WRIGHT/FL by Perrine; 1790 Census; FROST GEN, 74,75]

ABRAHAM 1 [John 2] b 1708 d Stephentown NY 1795. Cattlemark rec Cortlandt Manor 1766. Will 19 Mar 1791 proved 25 Nov 1795 names Benjamin, Martha, Abraham Jr dec'd, heirs of Sylvanus Raynor. Perh rec Stephentown WestCoNY 1790 w/3 in fam. Issue: Benjamin 1734, Martha 1744 m Joseph Osborne of Ridgefield NJ, Abraham Jr (dec'd), a dau (perh Amy) who m Sylvanus Raynor. [WRIGHT/FL by Perrine; SCJ, 264; 1790 Census]

ABRAHAM 2 [Abraham 1] d by 19 Mar 1791. Perh rec Stephentown WestCoNY 1790 w/9 in fam. Issue (from father's will): David, James both liv 1791. [WRIGHT/FL by Perrine; 1790 Census]

ABRAHAM 3 [Ebenezer] b Mansfield CT 13 Jul

1752 d Kingsbury NY 14 Feb 1814 m 1) 19 May 1773 **Sarah Babcock** d 1787 m 2) **Phebe Burt.** Lieut in NY Militia (Capt Wm Brown's co) in Rev. Leased lot in Berne AlbCoNY 1792. Issue: Ebenezer 1778, Esther. [DAR Lineage Book 123:43,240]

ABRAHAM 4 [Benjamin 1] b perh Yorktown NY 17 Mar 1758 d by 20 Feb 1843 m **Esther---**. Will proved 20 Feb 1843. [FROST GEN, 74]

ABRAHAM 5 [Daniel 13] b prob Berne, Albany Co NY 29 Aug 1804 d Barbourville, Delaware Co NY 17 Dec 1898 m 7 Oct 1827 **Lois Green** dau Robert & Naomi (Cummins) Green. [Private record, Mary K Witherbee]

ABRAHAM B 6 d Hackensack NJ, 30 Nov 1841, of Lodi, Bergen NY, m Fishkill NY, ca 16 Mar 1836 **Susan H Brinkerhoff** of Fishkill. Executors mortg land 1842. Issue (from will): Sarah Ann, Henrietta M (minors). [DutCoNY PR #3707, M:313; POUGHKEEPSIE M&D by Reynolds; DutCoNY Mortg 72:546]

ABRAHAM D 7 [Elijah 3] d Pleasant Valley NY 16 Oct 1848 (RR accident), m Pleasant Valley Pres Ch 22 Jan 1824 **Jane Allen** d 1850 dau Joseph of Po'keepsie. Will. Issue (from wills of Abraham and Wiltsey A): James Harvey 1831, John Reed 1831, Mary L, Jane Eliza, Jane Eliza (2nd), Wiltsey A d Louisiana 1 Aug 1857, Josephine, Sarah M. [DutCoNY PR (Abraham) #1891, (Wiltsey) #6063]

ABRAHAM 8 [Isaac 2] b 1809.

ABRAHAM 9 [Lewis 1] b 1826.

ABRAM 1 [Isaac 2] b Stormville, E Fishkill NY 8 Nov 1812 d Poughkeepsie NY 14 Sep 1900 m **Mary Warren.** 7 ch. [WRIGHT/FL by Perrine]

ABRAM 2 [James 20]

ABRAM 3 [James 16] b 1822.

ABRAM D 4 [Daniel 21] b 1852.

ADALINE 1 [Abel 1]

ADAM 1 [Peter 1] b 20 Mar 1650 d prob Oyster Bay LI 1698 m **Mary Dennis** d Oyster Bay LI 22 Jul 1698. Issue: Dennis 1673, Adam Jr, George, Joseph, Peter, Job. ["Wright Family," private MSS by Clara Wright Rathbun, Oneonta NY]

ADAM 2 [Dennis 1]. [WRIGHT/OB by Perrine]

ADAM 3 [Adam 1] of Oyster Bay b 1698. Will 23 11th Mo 1749 names ch Rachel, Deborah, Reuben, Abigail, gs Reuben, Solomon (under age). Issue: Rachel m John Frost, Deborah m Benjamin Farrington, Peter, Thomas, James 1721, Reuben, Solomon, Abigail. [NYCoNY PR 17:26 in NYHS 28:241; WRIGHT/OB by Perrine]

ADAM 4 [Joseph 1] d Norwich LI 1763 m **Elizabeth Kirk** dau Arthur & Temperance (Seaman) Kirk. Will 25 Dec 1762 proved 21 Feb 1763. Issue (from will): Sarah, Gilbert, Joseph, Almy, Benjamin, Deborah, William (under age). [NYCoNY PR 23:608 in NYHS 30:220]

ADAM 5 son [Joseph 2] of Westbury LI

ALANSON A 1 [Amasa 1] b CT ? 9 Feb 1790 d Rock Co WI betw 3 Mar 1868 and 2 Mar 1869 m 1815 **Sarah Wilcox** b 23 Feb 1795 d Rock Co WI 7 Dec 1873. To NY ae 9. Res Onondaga Co NY 1820. Later Beloit WI. Issue (b Onondaga Co NY): Randall 1819, Sidney 1820, Charlotte 1821, Sarah 1825, Alanson M 1832, Edward 1833, Sanford 1837. [Private record, Audrey Heise, Milwaukee WI]

ALANSON 2 [Jacob 11] b 1823.

ALANSON M 3 [Alanson 1] b 1832.

ALBERT 1 [William 22] b 1838 dy.

ALBERT H 2 [Abel 1]

ALFRED 1 [Enos 1]

ALFRED 2 [Jacob 11]

Alice (---) wf [Peter 1]

ALLISON 1 [Benjamin 3] butcher of NYC d by 27 Feb 1796 m (License) 7 Jul 1780 **Meliscent Halsey**. Adm 27 Feb 1796 to bro William, "friend" (bro/law) Jotham Post. Prob rec NYC 1790 w/4 in fam. [WRIGHT MARR, 49; NYCoNY PR in NYHS Vol 39; 1790 Census]

ALMY 1 dsp 1793 dau [Adam 4] of Oyster Bay

ALPHEUS 1 Rec Amenia DutCoNY 1790 w/4 in fam. [1790 Census]

ALVA 1 [John 46]

ALVAH K 2 [Joseph 16]

ALVIRA 1 [Cruger 1]

AMANDA 1 [William 25]

AMANDA 2 [Gilbert 5] b 1843.

Amanda (---) wf [Jacob 11]

AMASA 1 [Joshua 2]

AMBROSE 1 [George 4] b Saybrook CT 2 Oct 1773 d Wrightstreet, Durham GreCoNY 12 Jan 1851 m **Elizabeth Patterson**. Issue: Phila 1795, Caroline 1797, James 1799, Patterson 1801, Wealthy 1803, Ambrose Jr 1806, Ely 1808, Mary Jane 1810, William Clinton 1812, Zelia Diana 1815, Edwin 1817, Elizabeth 1819, Ezra 1821.

[CONE LINE by Cone; Private records of Ray Wright, Wheat Ridge CO]

AMBROSE 2 [Enos 1] b 1828.

AMBROSE 3 [George 4] b 1773.

AMBROSE JR 4 [Ambrose 1] b 1806.

AMBROSE PALMER 5 [David 10] b 1844.

AMELIA 1 [John 6] b perh Huntington LI 14 Apr 1734. [WRIGHT RECORDS by Stark]

AMELIA 2 [John 13] b 27 Apr 1767. [WRIGHT RECORDS by Stark]

Amelia (Baker) wf [Isaac 4]

AMY 1 [Dennis 1]. [WRIGHT/OB by Ferrine]

AMY 2 [? John 9] m (License) 28 Oct 1760 **Edward Colwell.**

AMY 3 [? Abraham 1] d by 2 May 1760 m **Sylvanus Raynor.** His will 2 May 1760 proved 2 Mar 1761 names bro Joseph, dau Martha ("Matthew Raynor, lately born of Ame Raynor decd"), exec Abraham Wright & uncle Samuel Raynor. Wife not proven, but Abraham Wright bequeathed to "heirs of Sylvanus Raynor." [NYCoNY PR 23:255 in NYHS Vol 30]

AMY 4 [James 4]

AMY 5 [Joseph 10]

Amy (Hazard) wf [Jonathan 5]
Amy (Mott) wf [Joseph 10]
Amy/Almy (Patterson) wf [James 4]

ANDERSON 1 [Lewis 1] b 1838.

ANGELINE 1 [Wise 2] b 1815.

ANGELINE 2 [Isaac 4] b 1817.

ANDREW 1 schoolmaster of Richmond Co NY d 1748 m **Mary---**. Will Dec 1747 proved 16 May 1747/8. Issue (from will): John, Jane (both under age). [NYCoNY PR 16:232 in NYHS 28:158]

ANNE 1 m (License) 24 Jun 1737 **Alexander Taylor**. [WRIGHT MARR,49]

ANN 2 m (License) 24 Sep 1755 **John Bennett**. [WRIGHT MARR,49]

ANNA 3 [William 1] b 9 Mar 1761 d Hopkinton NY 31 Oct 1826 m by 26 Dec. 1809, perh **Zebulon Mead** b Nine Partners NY 14 Mar 1753 d Hopkinton NY 27 Feb 1827 son Zebulon & Anna (Thompson) Mead. Ann Mead named in father's will. She prob m 2) **---Horton**. But see NANCY WRITE. [DutCoNY PR D:125; Query 5160-3 in *Connecticut Nutmegger* 11:474]

ANNE 4 [John 15] m 1) **Robert Cookes** m 2) **Joshua Hammond**. [WRIGHT/OB by Perrine]

ANN 5 m (License) 28 Aug 1778 **Timothy Prout**. [WRIGHT MARR,49]

ANNA [John 25] b 17 Jan 1785. See NANCY ANNA 2.

ANNA 6 [Daniel] b prob Clinton NY ca 1790, m 1) **John Ratner** m 2) **---Hubbard**. [Private rec, Mary K Witherbee, Oneonta NY (1979)]

ANN BELL 7 [William 4] b prob Flushing LI 17 Jul 1798 bp Flushing (St George's Ch) LI 29 Aug 1798. [St George's Ch Rec, in RECORD 112:42]

ANNA 8 [George 4] b 1763.

ANN 9 [George 5] b 1806.

ANN 10 [John 47]

ANNA A 11 [Joseph 10]

ANNA 12 [William 14]. Of Gallopsville NY.

ANN ELIZA 13 [Benjamin 12] b 1815.

ANN ELIZABETH 14 [Lewis 1] b 1830.

ANNA HALSTEAD 15 [John 38] b 1831.

ANNA MARIA 16 [Simon 1] b 1815.

Anne (---) wf [Charles 1]
Anne (---) wf [Nicholas 1]
Anna (Cunningham) wf [Justus 1]
Anna (Durland) wf [Elijah 1]
Ann (Henry) wf [Joseph 1]
Anna (Lay) wf [George 4]
Ann (Lord) wf [Nathaniel 9]
Anna (Sands) wf [Daniel 4]
Anna/Antje (Rol) wf [Jacob 3]

ANSON POST 1 [George 5] b 1792.

ANTHONY 1 [Nicholas 1] of Oyster Bay LI b Eng dsp by 8 Dec 1680 when will was proved. Deeded house in OB to sis-in-law Alice Crabbe and other "Quakers" 15 Oct 1672. Will 20 3rd Mo 1673 names sister "Alse Crabbe" primary legatee, bro Nicholas & Ann & son Caleb, and 2s6d each to Rebecca Frost, Sarah Lattin, John Wright, Gideon Wright & Elizabeth, Adam Wright & Mary, Job Wright, Mary Andrews, Jacob Townsend & Elizabeth, Lidia Wright, Richard Crab. [NYCoNY PR 1&2:400 in NYHS 25:105]

ANTHONY 2 [Job 1] d prob Staten Island NY ca 1746 m **Elizabeth**---. Will 22 Dec 1739 proved 10 Dec 1746. Issue (from will): Hendrick/Henry, Tabitha m a Mr. Randall (or Bondet per Perrine), Judith, Anthony (under age), Elizabeth, Zeborah, Mary (under 18), Hezekiah. Hezekiah, Joshua & Anthony Wright witn will of Wynant Winans 1732/3. [NYCoNY PR

16:58 (Anthony Wright) in NYHS 28:105; WRIGHT/OB by Perrine]

ANTHONY 3 [Gideon 1] b Oyster Bay LI 23 Nov 1686 d 10 Jul 1714 m **Mary Rhodes**. Issue: Peter 1703, Dinah 1705. [WRIGHT/OB by Perrine]

ANTHONY 4 [Anthony 2] b Staten Island NY d prob Worcester Co MD after 15 Jun 1761 m **Elizabeth Purnell**. His will 15 Jun 1761 names wf (co-exec), sons Zadok (under 18, land & marsh in Staten Island NY" lying between the property of my brother Hezekiah Wright and Bond Slack"..."also the ferry unto"), Hezekiah, Purnell, dau Mary, b/l Thomas Purnell (co-exec). Issue: Zadok, Mary, Purnell, Hezekiah. [Worcester Co MD PR 31:469, in *A Family History. Wright-Lewis-Moore and Connected Families. Early Settlers of Greene County, Georgia* by John Wright Boyd (Atlanta 1968), pp 36, 64]

ARISTEN 1 [Benjamin 7] b 1809.

AUGUSTINE 1 [John 6] b perh Huntington LI 25 May 1740. [WRIGHT RECORDS by Stark]

Augusta (Mead) wf [George 7]

AUGUSTUS 1 [David 6]

AUGUSTUS 1 [Jotham 2] b 1765.

AUSTIN READER 1 [David 6]

B

BALDWIN 1 [Solomon 3]

BARNABAS 1 [William 2] b 1769.

BARSHEBA 1 [Dennis 2] b 1763.

BARTOW 1 [Enos 1] b 1805.

BENJAMIN 1 [Abraham 1] b 13 Sep/Oct 1734 d 22 Nov 1823 ae 85 bur Yorktown (East Graveyard) NY m 22 May 1757 **Milicent Purdy** b 30 Jul/3 Oct 1735 d 25 Jun 1820 bur Yorktown NY. Farmer at Yorktown. Perh rec Stephentown WestCoNY 1790 w/5 in fam. Will dated 20 Jul 1812. Issue: Abraham 1758, Elizabeth 1761 ? m ----Hunt, Abijah 1763, Benjamin 1768, Martha 1771 m Joel Frost. [WRIGHT/FL by Perrine; NYS DAR Rec 7:317, copied by Joe V Wright; 1790 Census]

BENJAMIN 2 m (License) 1 May 1738 **Mary Smith** perh dau Benjamin Smith of Jamaica LI. Will of Benjamin Smith 1758 names Mary wf Benjamin Wright. [NYCoNY PR 21:286 in NYHS 29:305; WRIGHT MARR, 50]

BENJAMIN 3 [Jonathan 2] of Huntington LI d ca 1765 m **Elizabeth Allison/Ellison**. Will proved 18 Feb 1765. Issue (from will): Allison, William, Elizabeth 1757, Winifred m Jotham Post, Mary 1757, Charity m John Hallett, Sarah m Samuel Carman. [NYCoNY PR 27:347 in NYHS 31:344; WRIGHT/OB by Perrine]

BENJAMIN 4 [Benjamin 1] b 26 Nov 1768 d perh

21 Oct 1839 m 28 Apr 1790 **Elizabeth Beadle/Bedell** b 12 May 1771 d 23 May 1838 dau Ephraim & Philena (Frost) Beadle of Yorktown NY. Res Somers NY. Perh rec Bedford WestCoNY 1790 w/2 in fam. Issue: Joel 1793, Melicent 1796, Benjamin 1792, Ebenezer 1798, Philena aka Philo 1801, David 1805, Eliza 1811, Marron 1813. [WRIGHT/FL by Perrine; 1790 Census]

BENJAMIN 5 m (License) 7 Mar 1759 **Martha Fordham.** [WRIGHT MARR,50]

BENJAMIN JR 6 m **Elizabeth---.** Of Stephentown NY both mortg to Aug. VanCortland 1779. [DutCoNY Mortg F:34]

BENJAMIN 7 [David 5] b perh New Windsor NY 1774 d 1820 m **Jane Gregg.** Issue (partial): Aristen 1809. [David Wright lineage in DAR Rec]

BENJAMIN 8 [Adam 4] by by 1741, living 12 Dec 1783, named in will of bros Joseph of Jericho 1768 and Gilbert of Oyster Bay 1783. [NYCoNY PR 36:458 (Gilbert Wright) in NYHS 36:269]

BENJAMIN 9 [George 4] b 1780.

BENJAMIN 10 [Joseph 10] b 1805.

BENJAMIN 11 [Abijah 1] living 1812, named in will of gf Benjamin Wright. [WRIGHT/FL by Perrine]

BENJAMIN 12 [Benjamin 4] b prob Somers NY 6 Mar 1792 d 29 Sept 1858 m 10 Nov 1814 **Mary A Forman** b 6 Sept 1792 d 15 Dec 1855 dau Jacob & Jemima (Ryder) Forman. Issue: Ann Eliza 1815 m Dan C Miller, Catherine m Abraham H Miller, Forman dsp, Charlotte dsp, Susan dsp, Cordelia dsp. [WRIGHT/FL by Perrine; FROST GEN, 138; "Ryder Family Notes," in RECORD (1952) 83:230]

BENJAMIN BELDEN 13 [Isaac 2] b 1793. Of Cleveland OH.

BENJAMIN F 14 [David 10] b 1838.

BENJAMIN HALSTEAD 15 [John 38] b 1823.

BERIAH 1[Ephraim 1] b 1737.

Bethsheba (Frost) wf [Daniel 14]

BETSEY 1 [Daniel] b Albany Co NY ca 1796 prob d Wisconsin m **Ambrose Owen** d after 1850. Of Addison, Steuben Co NY. Issue: Diantha m ---Nichols res Wisconsin, Uri (twin), Uraline (twin).[Private rec, Mary K Witherbee (1979)]

BETSEY 2 [William 23]

Betsey (Hammond) wf [James 7]
Betsey (Langford) wf [Justus 2]

BRIDGETT 1 m (License) 25 Sept 1782 **Joseph Clark**. [WRIGHT MARR, 50]

Bridgett (Hallett) wf [Joseph 5]

C

CALEB 1 [Nicholas 2] b 1645 d Oyster Bay LI 1695 m **Elizabeth Dickinson** b 1652 d 1695. Issue: Elizabeth m Joseph Coles, Rebecca m John Underhill, Joseph, William 1680, Penelope m Daniel Reynolds. ["Ann Mott" by Hopper Striker Mott, in RECORD (1905), 36:60, 61; WRIGHT/OB by Perrine]

CALEB 2 [William 5] dsp Oyster Bay LI by 12 Feb 1753 m **Freelove Coles** dau Wright Coles. His will names wf, sis Sarah Wright, sis Mary Cooper, bro John Wright's chn (Baptist). Exec fath/law Wright Coles, bro-in-law Joseph Cooper, cousins Wm Townsend & Micajah Townsend. Proved 12 Feb 1753. [NYCoNY PR 18:233 in NYHS 28:421]

CALEB 3 [William 1] b 1755 dsp 1847. [WRIGHT/FL by Perrine]

CALEB 4 [? Robert 1] b 1 Jul 1774 [per Perrine] d 19 Aug 1853 ae 81 bur Carmel (Lake Mahapac Meth Ch) NY m New Castle NY 1797 **Mary Ann Cunningham** b 28 Aug 1772 d 20 Sep 1858 ae 86 bur Carmel dau Shubael/Hubal & Mariam (Mosher) Cunningham and twin of Marian Cunningham [qv]. Issue: Gilbert 1798, Green, Mary Ann m Budd Sloat, Sarah m David Travis, Stephen Thorn 1811, Eunice A m Harvey Newell Bayley. [PUTNAM COUNTY HIST by Pelletreau, 573; WRIGHT/OB by Perrine, 194; WESTCHESTER COUNTY HIST by Scharf, 1:678]

CALEB 5 of Cambridge AlbCoNY d by 22 Feb 1787. Adm to wid **Elizabeth---** of Cambridge. [Adm in NYHS 38:348]

CALEB 6 of Albany NY, m 20 Jul 1799 **Tirza Chapin.** [Albany (RDC) NY Rec]

CALEB 7 of Amenia NY prob b Mass say 1730 prob liv Amenia 1784. His gs Daniel Wright (of Weybridge VT son of Ebenezer) visited him there after 1784. [*History of Addison County VT*, 541]

CALEB 8 [Edmund 1]

CALEB 9 [Stephen 4] b 1833.

CALVIN 1 b ca 1765 d Esperance NY 3 Dec 1834 ae 78. Issue: John Calvin. [SCHOHARIE CO OBITS]

CAROLINE 1 [George 4] b 1766.

CAROLINE 2 [Ambrose 1] b 1797.

Caroline/Catherine (Phelps) wf WILLIAM 22
Catalina (---) wf [Jonas 1]

CATHERINE 1 [Jonathan 2] m **Jacob Griffin.** [WRIGHT/FL by Perrine]

CATHERINE 2 m (License) 22 Aug 1757 **John Nutt.** [WRIGHT MARR, 50]

CATHERINE 3 m (License) 6 Jan 1764 **Manasseh Salter.** [WRIGHT MARR, 50]

CATHERINE 4 [Samuel 3] b 19 Jan 1782 bp Flushing (St George's Ch) LI 29 Aug 1798. [St George's Ch Rec, in RECORD 112:42]

CATHERINE 5 [Benjamin 12]

CATHERINE 6 [William 14]

CATLEN 1 [John 17] b 1755.

Catherine (Blake) wf [Thomas 13]
Catherine (Fox) wf [Samuel 4]

Catherine (Pell) wf [Jacob 5]
Catherine (Rowe) wf [Jonathan 15]
Catherine (Thornton) wf [Samuel 14]

CHARITY 1 [Benjamin 3] m (License) 12 Apr 1780 **John Hallett**. [WRIGHT/OB by Perrine; WRIGHT MARR, 50]

Charity/Gerritje (---) wf [Elisha 1]
Charity (Bartow) wf [John 36]

CHARLES 1 [Jonathan 1] bp (adult) Jamaica (Grace Ch) LI 3 Mar 1727 m **Anne---**. Inherited homestead. Prob to Newtown LI by 1725/6 when he witn will of Constant Titus. Issue: Ruth 1727, perh Charles. [Private notes of Mary K Witherbee; Unrecorded will of Charles Titus, in NYHS 35:156]

CHARLES JR 2 [? Charles 1]. No further record. [notes of Mary K Witherbee]

CHARLES 3 m (License) 6 Nov 1764 **Susanna Palmer**. [WRIGHT MARR, 50]

CHARLES 4 [William 1] b 11 Dec 1762 d Philipstown NY 2 Aug 1830 bur North Highland Cem m 1787 **Sarah Mekell** dau Uriah Mekell of Philipstown NY. Rec Fishkill NY 1790. Will 30 Jul 1830 proved 7 Sep 1830. Issue: Haight 1787, Isaac 1790, James 1792, Uriah 1795, Sylvanus 1797, Thomas 1800, Frances 1802, Jemima 1806, William 1808, Elizabeth 1812. Perh rec Philipstown DutCoNY 1790 w/4 in fam. [Fishkill Reformed Ch Rec; WRIGHT/FL by Perrine; 1790 Census]

CHARLES 5 [Micaijah 1] b Somers Plains NY 1792 d Somers NY 1862 ae 70 m North Castle NY **Elizabeth Smith**. Res Lewisboro NY, then Somers NY. Issue: James, William Henry, John, Isaac Candee, Samuel Purdy. [WESTCHESTER COUNTY HIST by Scharf, 1:482; WRIGHT/FL by Perrine]

CHARLES 6 [Joseph 1] b perh Westbury LI by 13 Nov 1738 named in father's will.

CHARLES C 7 d Northeast NY 8 Jan 1842, leaving wf **Elizabeth---**, mother Meria Hanes, half sister Charity Hicks (wf of Lawrence), half bro John Hanes, half bro George Hanes. Purchaser of land (200 a) bordering CT 1824. Both sell (55 a) to Cyrus Swan of Sharon CT 1835. Wid mortg land in Northeast 1 Apr 1842. [DutCoNY PR #1710X; DutCoNY Mortg 72:570; DutCoNY Deeds 31:303, 55:239-243]

CHARLES 8 [Sylvanus 2] m **---Ludlam**. [WRIGHT/OB by Perrine]

CHARLES 9 [Isaac 6] b 1820.

CHARLES JACKSON 10 [John 38] b 1821.

CHARLES EMERSON 11 [George 7] b 1845.

CHARLES 12 [John 47]

CHARLOTTE 1 [Isaac 2], m **Samuel Colwell**, named in father's will 4 Mar 1842. [DutCoNY PR #3778]

CHARLOTTE 2 [John 38] b 1815.

CHARLOTTE 3 [Isaac 2]

CHARLOTTE 4 [Alanson 1] b 1821.

CHARLOTTE LOUISA 5 [George 7] b after 1850.

CHAUNCEY 1 son [Joseph 16]

Christian (Slaght) wf [Hezekiah 1]
Christina (Scott) wf [James 20]

CHRISTOPHER 1 [George 4] b 1776.

Clarissa (Curtiss) wf [Ebenezer 2]
Clement/Clemence (---) wf [David 1]

CORDELIA 1 [Benjamin 12]

CRUGER 1 b CT ca 1785 d Blendon, Franklin Co OH 5 Nov 1873 ae 78 bur Blendon (West Pioneer Cem) OH m **Abigail Goodrich** b CT d Blendon OH 17 Mar 1877 dau Bela & Abigail Goodrich. To Ohio 1808, soldier in War of 1812. Issue: Jeanette 1808 m Samuel Loomis, John 1810 dy, Lawrence 1818, Lauretta M 1820 m Perry Phelps, John G 1822, Alvira m George McWhirk. ["Inscriptions Blenton West Pioneer Cemetery," in *Old Northwest Genealogical Quarterly* 8:216-218]

Cynthia (Clarke) wf [James 11]

D

DANIEL 1 of Flushing LI, d by 28 Oct 1730 m **Deborah---** who adm est. [NYCoNY PR 11:1 in NYHS 27:1]

DANIEL 2 of Long Island had a son: Jacob 1747/8 [Query 3973-9, *Connecticut Nutmegger* 10:278]

DANIEL 3 [John 2] b prob Flushing LI 1708/17 d prob Cortlandt NY Mar 1781 perh m 1) **Keziah Sammis** m perh 2) **Rachel Horton** b prob Yorktown NY 1733 dau Daniel & Esther (Lane) Horton. Of Crum Elbow 1744-52, purchaser Cortland Manor 1762, with bro Jacob. Of Rumbout Pct NY mortgages 1770. "Capt Daniel Wright" in QueCo Militia 1758-61. Prob 2nd Reg't DutCo Militia under Capt Joseph Horton. Will 8 Feb 1777 proved 3 Mar 1781. (WRIGHT/OB by Perrine says he was son Edmund 2, that Keziah was his only wf, by whom a dau Elizabeth 1743 m Benjamin James of PA). Issue (from will): James, Daniel 1751, Esther 1761 m Enoch Knapp, Micajah 1764, Sarah m Jacob Frost, Fanny m Hazard Field of Yorktown, Hannah, Millicent 1770 m David Beadle, Rachel perh m ---Field, Phebe 1775 m Gilbert Haviland. [NYCoNY PR 33:265 in NYHS 33:240; DutCoNY Mortg 2:248, 5:137; Dutchess County Tax Lists; WRIGHT/FL by Perrine; SCJ, 372; DAR Patriot Index; HORTON GEN, 5; WRIGHT/OB by Perrine]

DANIEL 4 [Daniel 3] b 1751 d Smithtown LI by 23 Apr 1784 m **Anna (Sands) Thomas**. Adm 23 Apr 1784 to bro Micajah. Issue: "only dau" Glorianna 1774. [NYHS 36:415 (Daniel Wright Adm); WestCoNY Wills A:152 (Gloria);

WRIGHT/FL by Perrine]

DANIEL 5 [Earl 1] b Middletown CT 19 Jan 1752 d Maryland OtsCoNY 16 Mar 1840 m Chatham NY Nov 1778 **Lovina Sutherland** b 1764. Enlisted at Kinderhook NY. 1834 OtsCoNY Pension List. Partial issue: Rhoda 1780 m Roger Kelley, Thomas 1785. [WRIGHT MARR, 51; DAR Lineage Bk 32:275, 76:373]

DANIEL 6 [Ephraim 1] b Hebron CT 1756 d Westport NY 1 Oct 1822 m **Patience Bill**. Col John Stark's NH Militia 1775. Issue (partial): Jerusha m 1793 Elias Sturtevant. [ABEL WRIGHT GEN by Stephen Wright; DAR Lineage Bk 86:78; *Descendants of Samuel Sturtevant* by Robert Sturtevant (Waco TX 1986) p 6-12]

DANIEL 7 Beekman NY Tax List Jun 1746-Feb 1758. [Beekman Tax Lists]

DANIEL 8 of Crum Elbow Pct NY deeds to Jacob Elliott of Voluntown CT 7 May 1755. [DutCoNY Deeds 3:224,225]

DANIEL 9 Nine Partners tax list Feb 1753-Jun 1760. [CRUM ELBOW TAX LISTS]

DANIEL 10 Northeast tax list Jun 1760-1769. [CRUM ELBOW TAX LISTS]

DANIEL 11 Poughkeepsie tax list Jun 1766-Jun 1767 [CRUM ELBOW TAX LISTS]

DANIEL 12 "Right" of Rombout mortgaged to Derick Brinkerhoff, 14 Jan 1769; perh again or similar 2 Dec 1786. [DutCoNY Mortg 2:248, 5:137]

DANIEL 13 b prob DutCoNY (per son's recollection) d Smithville Flats, Chenango Co NY 1815 m prob Dutchess Co NY by 1790 **Mary Nelson** prob dau Mephibosheth & Merriam Nelson of Little Nine Partners NY. Perh Daniel

"Right" of Clinton NY 1790, Berne NY 1800, Smithville Flats NY 1810. Leased Lot 542 Rensselaerwyck Manor, Berne 8th mo 1792, sold W 1/2 to Stephen Wright 1802. Issue: Anna ca 1790 m 1) John Ratner m 2) ---Hubbard, Justus ca 1790/1, Margaret m ---Hubbard, Betsey ca 1796 m Ambrose Owen, Meriam ca 1796 m John Carhart, David ca 1798, Daniel Jr ca 1802, Abraham 1804, Isaac (twin) 1804. [Private rec, Mary K Witherbee; 1790 & 1800 Census]

DANIEL 14 [Edmund 1] of Oyster Bay m Jamaica (Grace Ch) LI 5 May 1711 **Eliphal Townsend** dau John & Mary (Townsend) Wright. No issue. See Eliphal Wright. [GRACE CH by Ladd]

DANIEL 15 [Thomas 9] b 23 Aug bp Fishkill (Hopewell Reformed Ch) DutCoNY 29 Sep 1782. [Hopewell Reformed Ch Rec]

DANIEL 16 [Zebulon 1] of Oyster Bay m **Sarah Walters**. Issue: Freelove m Benjamin Latting, Abigail m Adolphus Latting, Martha m Levi Cock, Horace/Horatio, Samuel 1763, Daniel. [UNDERHILL GEN, 138; WRIGHT/OB by Perrine]

DANIEL 17 of Dutchess Co NY m by 1780 **Sarah---** and had issue: Walter who m 1802. Perh "Daniel Jr" rec Fishkill 1790 w/4 in fam. [Pleasant Valley NY Presby Ch Rec; 1790 Census]

DANIEL 18 [Micaijah 1] b prob Stephentown WestCoNY 21 Nov 1790 d 12 May 1864. [WRIGHT/FL by Perrine]

DANIEL C 19 [Robert 1] b 11 Jan 1797 d Somers WestCoNY 17 Oct 1873 bur Ivandale Cem m 1818 **Mary Slote** dau Charles & Susan Sloat of Union Valley NY. Res Somers NY. Issue: Elias 1819, Leonard Slote 182-, Eliza Jane 1823. [WRIGHT/FL by Perrine]

DANIEL 20 of New Hackensack DutCoNY, m by 21 Jul 1801 **Mary Jeacocks**, and had issue: Sarah bp 1802. [New Hackensack RDC Rec]

DANIEL 21 [Walter 1] b Schoharie Co NY ca 1805 m **Wilhelmina---**. Rec 1835 Carlisle SchCoNY, 1850 Richmondville SchCoNY, 1855 Richmondville. Both sell Lot 14 Carlisle 1836. Both buy Lot 49 Skinner Patent Carlisle (later Richmondville) NY 1836 and sell same 1851 to Demosthenes & Walter Wright. Issue (from Census): Eliza ca 1828, Walter 1833, Emma 1840, Louisa 1840, Olive 1844, Margaret J 1846, John C 1848, Julia 1848, Abram D 1852.
[SchCoNY Deeds V:65, V:72, 30:501, 32:449; 1850 Federal & 1855 NY State Census]

DANIEL I 22 [Isaac 2] b Stormville, E Fishkill NY 5 Feb 1791 d prob Delhi NY living 1842, named in father's will. Methodist circuit rider. Issue: William and perh others. [WRIGHT/FL by Perrine; Mary K Witherbee (1979) notes]

DANIEL JR 23 [Daniel 13] b Albany Co NY ca 1802 m 1) Steuben Co NY **Abbie Cunningham** m 2) **Roxana Crowl**. [Private rec of Mary K Witherbee]

DANIEL 24 [Daniel 15] d 1819 m **Phebe Bennett** of LI. [WRIGHT/OB by Perrine]

DANIEL 25 [Edmund 1]. See ELIPHAL

DANIEL 26 [Edmund 2]

DANIEL 27 [Matthew 1]

DAVID 1 [Jonathan 1] bp (RDC New York, adult) 12 Dec 1694 d Flushing LI by 27 Apr 1721 living 30 Jul 1718 m 1) **Hannah Thurston** dau Joseph & Anne Thurston m 2) **Clement/ Clemence---** who survived him and deposed as his widow 27 Apr 1721. Justice of Peace QueCoNY 1710-18. Will of Anne Thurston 1715 (proved 1721) mentions Hannah wf David

Wright. Issue: David Jr, Phebe. [WRIGHT/FL by Perrine; Mary K Witherbee notes (1979)]

DAVID 2 [David 1] b by 1698 lived at Flushing LI. Issue: David 1732, perh Nathaniel. [notes by Mary K Witherbee (1979)]

DAVID 3 [David 2] b 1732. Res Hempstead LI. Issue: David 1752, John 1753, Nathaniel, Samuel, perh Silas. [WRIGHTS OF LONG ISLAND by Francis Wright]

DAVID 4 [David 3] b Hempstead NY 22 Jul 1752 d by 14 Nov 1838 m by 1783 **Mary---** when both ("then of New Windsor NY") sold land on LI to bro Nathaniel. Served Ulster Co militia. Res Little Britain, New Windsor OraCoNY and, after 1820, Warwick NY. Carpenter. Witn 1813 to will of bro John Wright. Issue: Joseph, John 1786, Elizabeth m ---Keeler, Nathaniel. See DAVID 5. [WRIGHTS OF LONG ISLAND by Francis Wright]

DAVID 5 of New Windsor NY, b 1745 d 1833 m 1) ---- m 2) 1773 **Margaret Woodhull**. Pvt "David Right" in Col James McClaughrey's 2nd Ulster Co NY Co. Issue: Benjamin 1774, Nathaniel, Joel, Deri--, Elizabeth m ---Horton, Hannah m David Vance, Sara perh (but doubtful) m Capt. Charles Halstead. Perh rec New Windsor UlstCoNY 1790 w/9 in fam. See DAVID 4. [DAR Lineage Book 119:59,60; 1790 Census]

DAVID 6 [Jotham 3] b near Peekskill NY 14 Dec 1779 d Newburgh, Orange Co NY 29 Aug 1835 m **Temperance Reader**, b ca 1791 d Newburgh NY 1848 ae 57 (obit 29 Apr 1848). His will 23 Aug 1835 proved 11 Nov 1835. Issue (from will): Eliza 1809 m Joshua Marston, William 1813, Mary 1815, Austin Reader 1819, John 1821, Gabriel 1824, David Jr 1827, Elias Gedney 1832, Augustus. [OraCoNY PR J:351; WRIGHTS OF LONG ISLAND by Francis Wright; Deaths from Poughkeepsie Newspapers, abstracted by Clifford M. Buck (1979)]

DAVID 7 [Abraham 2] living 1791, named in will of gf Abraham Wright. [WRIGHT/FL by Perrine]

DAVID 8 of Schoharie, b ca 1791, d Schoharie NY 7 Apr 1851 ae about 60. [SCHOHARIE CO OBITS]

DAVID 9 [Daniel 13] b prob Berne NY ca 1798 d Binghamton NY 1871 m **Phebe Brown**. Will 14 Dec 1870 proved 1 Jul 1871. Issue: Elisha, Erastus, Margaret, Samantha, Edward, Eunice. [BroomeCoNY PR; Private rec of Mary K Witherbee]

DAVID 10 [? William 10] b Berne NY ca Sep 1801 d Schoharie NY 7 Apr 1865 ae 63-6-7 bur Schoharie (Old Stone Fort Cem) NY m 1) ca 1823 **Phebe Gardiner** b ca 1803 d 1848 bur So Berne (Wright Burying Ground) NY dau Daniel & Mercy (Burtch) Gardner m 2) Wright NY 29 Oct 1848 **Mary (Wood) Eaton**. Rec Berne NY 1830-1840, Schoharie NY 1850-1860. Sold remainder of Lot 523 Berne 1848. Issue (b Berne): James Harvey 1824, Sally Ann, Rebecca, Perry Gardner 1830, William D 1833, Philo Bradley 1834, Joseph C 1835, Benjamin F 1838, Melbourn O 1840, Hemen Gardner 1842, Ambrose Palmer, Phebe Gardner 1848. [AlbCoNY Deeds 31:246, 97:411, 70:280, 78:179; "Benjamin F. Wright," in *Portrait and Biographical Record of Walworth and Jefferson Counties, Wisconsin*, 218]

DAVID 11 [Benjamin 4] b 1805.

DAVID 12 [Gilbert 5] b 1826.

DAVID 13 [David 6] b 1827.

DAVID 14 [Stephen 4] b 1840.

DEBORAH 1 [Samuel 1] bp Newtown (Presby Ch) LI 8 Jan 1738 perh same who m Newtown (Presby Ch) 29 Dec 1749 **Samuel Leverich**. [WRIGHT/FL by Perrine; Newtown Presby Ch Rec]

DEBORAH 2 [Adam 3] m 6 Apr 1737 **Benjamin Farrington** of LI. [WRIGHT/OB by Perrine]

DEBORAH 3 [Nicholas 2]

DEBORAH 4 [Adam 4]

DEBORAH 5 [William 2] b 1768.

DELILAH 1 [Robert 2] b 21 Feb 1810 m **Smith Austin Dean**. [WRIGHT/FL by Perrine]

DELILAH 2 [William 13] b 1827.

Delilah (Kronk) wf [John 43]

DEMOSTHENES L 1 [? Walter 1] With bro Elijah & Walter Jr mortgages land in SchCoNY 1850. With same buys of Daniel Wright 1851 land in Richmondville NY. [SchCoNY Deeds 21:441, Mortg W:179]

DENA 1 [John 16]

DENNIS 1 [Adam 1] b 1673 d 1753 bur Huntington (Episc Ch) LI m 1699 **Susannah Hawkhurst**. Issue: Dennis 1711, Amy, Uriah, Elizabeth, Adam. ["Wright Family," private MSS by Clara Wright Rathbun, Oneonta NY]

DENNIS 2 [Dennis 1] b perh Oyster Bay LI ca 1711 d 1798 m 1739 **Susannah (Stephens) Smith**. Of Westport CT. Leased farm in Patterson NY 1762. Of Fredericksburgh NY (age 58) on 30 Dec 1769 lease. Issue: Obadiah, Freelove, Mary, Hannah, Dennis ca 1760, Elizabeth, Barsheba ca 1763. [PUTNAM COUNTY HIST by Pelletreau, 642, 635; "Wright Families" private MSS by Clara Wright Rathbun, Oneonta NY]

DERIUS 1 [Jonathan 12] b 1768 prob d young. [NYS DAR Bible Record, 46:100]

DERIUS? 2 [David 5] perh of New Windsor NY. [DAR Lineage Book 119:59]

DERYCK 1 [John 36] b 1785.

DESIAR/DESIRE [Ephraim 2] b perh Kent NY 18 Feb 1790. [WRIGHT RECORDS by Stark]

DIADEMIS m Fishill NY 31 Nov 1795 **John Carman**. [Fishkill Reformed Ch Rec]

DINAH 1 [Anthony 3] b 705.

DINA 2 [Elisha 1] b 17 Mar 1804 bp Berne (St Paul Evang Luth Ch) NY 17Jun 1804. [St Paul Evang Luth Ch Rec]

DORCAS [James 20] b 1822.

E

EARL 1 b Middletown CT 1726 d Otsego Co NY 1810. Pvt 1777 in Capt John Smith's Co Col Abraham Van Alstine's Reg't AlbCoNY Militia. Partial issue: Daniel 1752. [DAR Lineage Bk 76:373]

EARL 2 [Matthew 1]

EBENEZER 1 [Robert 1] b ca 1763 d Carmel (Presby Ch) NY 9 July 1806 ae 43 m **Rachel---** d 27 Oct 1829 ae 66. Perh rec Frederickstown DutCoNY 1790 w/5 in fam. Adm to widow 28 Aug. 1806. [DutCoNY PR #438; 1790 Census]

EBENEZER 2 [Abraham 3] b 1778 d 1863 m 1) --- m 2) 1824 **Clarissa Curtiss**. Issue (partial): William Woodworth 1825. [DAR Lineage Book 123:43,240]

EBENEZER 3 of Albany? NY, b ca 1784 d 14 Aug 1854 ae 72. [Munsell's *Annals of Albany*, Vol 9]

EBENEZER 4 [Benjamin 4] b prob Somers NY 19 Aug 1798 d 25 Aug 1862 m **Nancy B Green**. [WRIGHT/FL by Perrine]

EBENEZER 5 [John 35] b Westerlo NY ca 1800 m **Susan Briggs**. Res Quaker Street, Duanesburg NY. [Howell, Tenney, & Munsell's *Albany and Schenectady Counties* (1886), Pt 2, 167]

EBENEZER 6 [Robert 2] b 9 Mar 1807 d 1881. [WRIGHT/FL by Perrine]

EBENEZER 7 [Matthew 1]

EBENEZER 8 [John 42] d 1848.

EBER 1 [Wise 2]

EDMOND 1 [Nicholas 1] of Oyster Bay b 1640 d 1703 m **Sarah Wright** b 1648 dau Peter & Alice Wright. Issue: Nicholas, Caleb, Edmund, Daniel, Jacob, Sarah m Samuel Birdsall. [WRIGHT/OB by Perrine]

EDMOND 2 [Edmund 1] b Oyster Bay LI 1670 d Oct 1733 m Oyster Bay LI 1695 **Sarah Townsend**. Will 2 Dec 1731 proved 3 Nov 1733, exec James Dickenson. Issue (from will): Nicholas, Jotham, Daniel, Thomas, Edmund, Jacob, Zerviah/Zeraiah m John Wright. [WRIGHT MARR, 51; NYCoNY PR 12:96 in NYHS 27:126; WRIGHT/OB by Perrine]

EDMUND 4 [Edmund 2] dsp Oyster Bay 1750. Joiner. Will 25 May 1750 proved 21 Dec 1750 naming bros Nicholas, Daniel. [NYCoNY PR 17:265 in NYHS 28:308]

EDMUND 5 farmer of South East NY, witn 25 Mar 1784 to will of Benjamin Sears. [NYHS 38:113]

EDMUND 6 [Isaac 7]

EDWARD 1 [Robert 2] b 31 Mar 1804 d 14 Feb 1890 perh m **Sarah Read**. [WRIGHT/FL by Perrine]

EDWARD 2 [Robert 2] b 1804.

EDWARD 3 [John 42] b 1826.

EDWARD 4 [Alanson 1] b 1833.

EDWARD 5 [Joseph 16]

Electa (Shed) wf [Thomas 12]

ELY 1 [Ambrose 1] b 1808.

ELI 2 [Gilbert 4] b 1831.

ELIAS 1 [Daniel 19] b 1819.

ELIAS GEDNEY 2 [David 6] b 1832.

ELIJAH 1 [Gideon 2] b Oyster Bay 4 Apr 1713 d Nov 1766 m Oyster Bay 1742 **Anna Durland** dau John & Mary (Birdsall) Durland. Will of "Garitt Durling" 1758 names "sister Ann Wright." Elijah's will of Norwich, Oyster Bay LI 31 Oct 1766 proved 31 Dec 1766. Exec "friend and neighbor" John Wright, "kinsman" Fry Willis. Issue (from will): Gideon 1751, Freelove m 1) Samuel Wood 2) Samuel Nichols. Also Mary d by Oct 1766, Zebulon d by Oct 1766. [NYCoNY PR 21:1 (Durling), 25:435 (Wright) in NYHS 29:229, 31:53; WRIGHT RECORDS by Stark; WRIGHT/OB by Perrine; *The Dorland Family in America* by John Dorland Cremer (1898), 48]

ELIJAH 2 b ca 1746 d Carmel (Presby Ch) NY 17 Jul 1815 ae 69. Perh rec Frederickstown DutCoNY 1790 (1-3-2). Acct with Dr Cornelius 10 Apr 1794 to 31 Dec 1803 names "wf, inf, Margarett, dau, son chn." Issue (among others): Margarett. [PUTNAM COUNTY HIST by Pelletreau, 573; 1790 Census]

ELIJAH 3 b ca 1770 d Pleasant Valley NY 15 Apr 1837, m **Mary---** bp (adult) Pleasant Valley Presby Ch 22 Aug 1813, d 7 Jul 1850 ae 88. Issue (from his will): Abraham D, Joseph, Mary. Also named: gs Elijah Belden Lattin. [DutCoNY PR #3519; J:485]

ELIJAH 4 b ca 1782 d 11 Nov 1827 ae 45 bur Carmel (Hughson Farm Cem) NY. [PUTNAM COUNTY HIST by Pelletreau, 573]

ELIJAH 5 [Ephraim 2] b perh Kent NY 26 Jan 1793. [WRIGHT RECORDS by Stark]

ELIJAH 6 [? Walter 1] With bro Walter Jr and

Demosthenes mortg land in SchCoNY 15 Mar 1850. [SchCoNY Mortg W:179.

ELIJAH 7 [Ephraim 2] b 1793.

ELIPHAL 1 [John 1] prob b Oyster Bay LI m 1) **Henry Townsend** d 4 Sep 1709 son Henry & Deborah (Underhill) Townsend m 2) (license) Jamaica (Grace Ch) LI 5 May 1711 **Daniel Wright** [14] son Edmund of Oyster Bay who dsp m 3) **John Morris**. Issue (by Townsend): Henry, Absolom 1708, (by Morris) Deborah, Justus, John. [UNDERHILL GEN, 1:86; *Winthrop-Babcock Genealogy*, 572; GRACE CH by Ladd]

ELISHA 1 [John 22] b prob Dutchess Co NY ca 1778 living Berne AlbCoNY 1850 m perh Berne NY by 1800 **Gerritje/Charity---** living 1850. Rec Berne NY 1800. Purchaser Schoharie NY (Lot 28) 1833, mortgaged 1833, sold 1838. Sold 1/5 of Lot 501, Berne AlbCoNY, to Matthew Strevel 1838. Issue (among others): Dina 1804. [SchCoNY Deeds Q:339, V:65, Mortg I:364; AlbCoNY Deeds 61:114]

ELISHA CROMWELL 2 [Solomon 3]

ELIZA 1 [Benjamin 1768] b prob Somers NY 13 Apr 1811 d 22 May 1862. [WRIGHT/FL by Perrine]

ELIZA 2 [Jotham 3] b Peekskill NY 10 May 1780 m **William Willson** of Pine Plains DutCoNY. [WRIGHT/OB by Perrine]

ELIZA 3 [Simon 1] b 1804.

ELIZA 4 [David 6] b 1809.

ELIZA 5 [Benjamin 4] b 1811.

ELIZA 6 [Daniel 21] b 1828.

ELIZA 7 [John 47]

ELIZA ANN 8 [Abel 1]

ELIZA ANN 9 [William 24]

ELIZA JANE 10 [Daniel 19] b 1823.

ELIZA MOORE 11 [John 38] b 1834.

Eliza (Southwick) wf [Joseph 18]

ELIZABETH 1 [Dennis 1]

ELIZABETH 2 [Gideon 1] m **Isaiah Harrison**. [WRIGHT/FL by Perrine]

ELIZABETH 3 [Gideon 2] b Oyster Bay LI 5 Apr 1703. [WRIGHT RECORDS by Stark]

ELIZABETH 4 [Jonathan 2] m ---Wheeler. [WRIGHT/FL by Perrine]

ELIZABETH 5 [John 5] m **Edmond Weeks**. ["Early Ludlam...Families", in *TAG* 14:8]

ELIZABETH 6 [John 9]. No further record. [WRIGHT/FL by Perrine]

ELIZABETH 7 [Henry 2] bp Fishkill RDC 1731. [Fishkill RDC Rec]

ELIZABETH 8 [Caleb 1] m **Joseph Coles**. [WRIGHT/OB by Perrine]

ELIZABETH 9 m (License) 9 Nov 1738 **Jacob Rickew**. [WRIGHT MARR, 51]

ELIZABETH 10 m (License) 28 Jul 1753 **John Valentine**. [WRIGHT MARR, 51]

ELIZABETH 11 m (License) 14 Jul 1756 **Abraham Sleeth**. [WRIGHT MARR, 51]

ELIZABETH 12 m (License) 31 Aug 1758 **Jasper Allen**. [NY State Colonial Records, quoted in WRIGHT MARR, 51

ELIZABETH 13 [Reuben 2] m **Jesse Hallock**. Issue: Wright. [WRIGHT/FL by Perrine]

ELIZABETH 14 [Benjamin 1] m ---**Hunt**. Note: Frost says it was her bro Abijah who m ---Hunt. [WRIGHT/FL by Perrine; FROST GEN, 75]

ELIZABETH 15 m (License) 28 Nov 1757 **Jeremiah Blanck**. [WRIGHT MARR, 51]

ELIZABETH 16 m (License) 28 Jul 1760 **William Scott**. [WRIGHT MARR, 51]

ELIZABETH 17 m (License) 23 Jun 1761 **Abraham VanWyck**. [WRIGHT MARR, 51]

ELIZABETH 18 m (License) 25 Mar 1765 **Benjamin James**. [WRIGHT MARR, 51]

ELIZABETH 19 [John 13] b 2 May 1772. [WRIGHT RECORDS by Stark]

ELIZABETH 20 [David 4] perh b New Windsor NY m ---**Keeler**. [WRIGHTS OF LONG ISLAND by Francis Wright]

ELIZABETH 21 [Samuel 10] b 29 Apr 1779, m **Thomas Hayes**. Elizabeth Hays named in father's 1831 will. [Private rec of Joe V Wright, Haverford Pa]

ELIZABETH 22 [Joseph 12] b Fishkill NY 28 Jan 1781. [Fishkill RDC Rec]

ELIZABETH 23 [Thomas 2] m (License) 6 Feb 1783 **William Wright**. See William 8. [WRIGHT MARR, 52]

ELIZABETH 24 [Jacob 2] m WestCoNY 21 Mar 1787 **Seth Whitney**. [WRIGHT MARR, 52]

ELIZABETH 25 m East Chester NY 1795 **Stephen Wright**. See Stephen 2. [NY MARR, 52]

ELIZABETH 26 [Micajah 1] b prob Stephentown WestCoNY 31 Mar 1794 d 10 May 1863 m 23 May 1812 **James Phillips** of Danbury CT. 3 children. [WRIGHT/FL by Perrine]

ELIZABETH 27 [Ephraim 2] b perh Kent NY 1 Nov 1794. [WRIGHT RECORDS by Stark]

ELIZABETH 28 [Robert 2] b 17 Jul 1799 d 26 Jan 1882 m **Eleazer Ferguson** of Delaware Co NY. [WRIGHT/FL by Perrine]

ELIZABETH 29 m prob Dutchess Co NY by 10 Jan 1804 **John J VanWyck**. Issue (bp Hopewell Reformed Ch 28 Nov 1814): Cornelis 1804, Jane 1805, Maria 1807, Alanson 1814 d young, Alanson (2nd) 1816. [Hopewell Reformed Ch Rec]

ELIZABETH 30 [Charles 4] b perh Philipstown NY 1 Jan 1812 d 25 Aug 1884 m 1) **Charles Colwell** m 2) **Herman Goodsell**. [WRIGHT/FL by Perrine]

ELIZABETH 31 [Abijah 1] living 1812, named in will of gf Benjamin Wright. [WRIGHT/FL by Perrine]

ELIZABETH 32 m Fishkill NY 29 Jan 1814 **John VanVleek/VanVlack** prob son George VanVlack. Issue: Aaron. [Fishkill Reformed Ch Rec; *Transcript*, Query 8100, 46 Apr 1920]

ELIZABETH 33 [Isaac 2], named in his will 1842.

ELIZABETH 34 [Daniel 3] b 1743.

ELIZABETH 35 [Benjamin 3] b 1757.

ELIZABETH 36 [Samuel 4] b 1786.

ELIZABETH 37 [Ephraim 2] b 1794.

ELIZABETH 38 [George 5] b 1802.

ELIZABETH 39 [Isaac 4] b 1811.

ELIZABETH 40 [Ambrose 1] b 1819.

ELIZABETH 41 [Gilbert 5] b 1822.

ELIZABETH 42 [Isaac 6] b 1836.

ELIZABETH 43 [Anthony 2]

ELIZABETH 44 [David 5]

ELIZABETH 45 [Gideon 4]

ELIZABETH 46 [Isaac 2]

ELIZABETH 47 [John 15

ELIZABETH 48 [Job 1]

ELIZABETH 49 [Robert 4]

ELIZABETH 50 [William 14]

Elizabeth (---) wf [Adam 4]
Elizabeth (---) wf [Benjamin 6]
Elizabeth (---) wf [Caleb 5]
Elizabeth (---) wf [Charles 7]
Elizabeth (---) wf [Jonathan 8]
Elizabeth (---) wf [Samuel 3]
Elizabeth (Allison) wf [Benjamin 3]
Elizabeth (Bailey) wf [James 5]
Elizabeth (Banker) wf [Thomas 9]
Elizabeth (Beadle) wf [Benjamin 4]
Elizabeth (Carpenter) wf [John 13]
Elizabeth (Cooper) wf [Thomas 2]
Elizabeth (Dickinson wf [Caleb 1]
Elizabeth (Dusenbury) wf [Jotham 3]
Elizabeth (Haight) wf [Jacob 2]
Elizabeth (Kirk) wf [Adam 4]
Elizabeth (Lee) wf [James 3]
Elizabeth (Lee) Curry wf [Robert 1]
Elizabeth (Patterson) wf [Ambrose 1]
Elizabeth (Post) wf [George 5]
Elizabeth (Purnell) wf [Anthony 4]

Elizabeth (Grosbeck) Rochell wf [Thomas 2]
Elizabeth (Shed) wf [Peter 5]
Elizabeth (Smith) wf [Charles 5]
Elizabeth (Townsend) wf [Gideon 1]
Elizabeth (Wright) wf [Gilbert 5]

ELMIRA 1 [Richard 2]

ELVIN 1 [Joseph 16] b 1827 dy.

Emeline (---) wf [Joseph 20]
Emeline Palelia (Peak) wf [Joseph 21]

EMMA 1 [Daniel 21] b 1840.

ENOS 1 [William 1] b Philipstown NY 15 Apr 1772 d Fishkill NY 17 Jun 1855 ae 83 bur Fishkill (RDC yard) NY m 1) prob Bedford NY 15 Jan 1799 **Miriam Woolsey** d 15 Jan 1822 m 2) Fishkill NY 7 Aug 1823 **Abigail Whittemore** b 1788 d 25 Jul 1862 ae 74 bur Fishkill (RDC yard) NY. Exec of father's will 1809. Will 20 Jun 1837 names issue: Theodore A, Alfred, Bartow 1805, William W, Hannah 1813 m William Anthony, Mary 1802/3 m Wm Anthony. Also Elizabeth 1800/10, Woolsey, Ambrose 1828, Josiah W 1821 (not named). Will also names bro Caleb. [DutCoNY PR #4615, S:437; POUGHKEEPSIE M&D by Reynolds; WRIGHT/FL by Perrine; "Bartow Wright MD" in *History of Orange County, NY*; FISHKILL TOMBSTONES]

ENOS 2 [William 14]

EPHRAIM 1 [Abel 1] b Lebanon CT 29 Feb 1704 d ca 1759 m 29 Jun 1724 **Hannah Wood** who d 18 Mar 1737. Issue: John 1726, Hannah 1831, Martha 1733, Ephraim 1735, Ann (twin) 1735, Beriah 1737, Daniel 1756. [ABEL WRIGHT by Stephen Wright]

EPHRAIM 2 [John 13] b perh Kent NY 6 Feb 1766 m 1) **Martha Fuller** b 8 Aug 1770 d 6 June 1796 m 2) by 7 Oct 1811 **Lucy Pratt** b 24 May 1770. Of Frederickstown NY by 1811 when he and Lucy mortgaged 52 a in Frederickstown. Issue (from Gideon Wright's Acct Book and a Bible Rec): John 1788, Deziar 1790, Elijah 1793, Elizabeth 1794, John Pratt 1797. [WRIGHT RECORDS by Stark; Query #8081, in *Transcript* 28 Feb 1934; DutCoNY Mortg 17:29]

EPHRAIM 3 [Ephraim 1] b 1735.

ERWIN 1 [Jacob 11]

ESTHER 1 [Abraham 3] [DAR Lineage Book 123:240]

ESTHER 2 [Daniel 3] b Yorktown NY Sept 1761 m WestCoNY 25 Jan 1787 **Enoch Knapp**. Issue (b Yorktown): Prudence 1788, Esther m Charles Bliven, Allen, James. [SCJ, 372; WRIGHT MARR, 52; FROST GEN, 339; HORTON GEN, 13]

ESTHER 3 [John 16]. No further record. [DUTCHESS COUNTY HIST, 498]

ESTHER 4 of Clinton NY d by 4 Feb 1793 m by 1789 **Wright S Skinner** b 1760/70 living 1830. He m 2) by 4 Feb 1793 **Hannah TenEyck** and rec Clinton NY 1790, Berne NY 1800-1810, Camden NY 1830. He leased Lot 543 Berne, about 1809 sold 145 1/2 a in Coeymans NY to Stephen Willes. Issue (by Esther bp Linlithgo (RDC) NY): Sarah 1789. Issue (by Hannah): John 1795, Christina 1796, Robert 1797, Christopher 1799, Martha 1800, Francis 1801, William 1803, Reuben, and prob Esther m 1829 John A Weidman. [Linlithgo Reformed Ch Rec; Beaver Dam Ch Rec, St Paul's Evang Luth Ch Rec].

ESTHER 5 [Matthew 1]

Esther (Horton) wf [Simeon 5]
Esther (Lewis) wf [Matthew 1]
Ethelannah (Frost) wf [Jonathan 12]

EUNICE 1 [Samuel 4] b 1788.

EUNICE A 2 [Caleb 4]

EZRA 1 [Ambrose 1] b 1821.

EZRA 2 [Stephen 4] b 1835.

EZRA 3 [Richard 2]

F

FANNY L 1 [William 4] b 1798/1810 bp Flushing (St George's Ch) LI 5 May 1810 m Flushing (St George's Ch) 25 Feb 1834 **George Wallace Birck**. [St George's Ch Rec, in RECORD, 110:67, 112:45]

FANNY 2 [James 4]

FANNY 3 [John 35]

FANNY 4 [Wise 2] b 1802.

FORMAN 1 [Benjamin 12]

FRANCES 1 aka Fanny [Daniel 3] d Yorktown NY 15 Jan 1795 m Yorktown NY 9 Jun 1788 **Hazard Field** b 11 Nov 1764 d Yorktown NY 1815 son John & Lydia Field. [WRIGHT/FL by Perrine; WRIGHT MARR, 52; FROST GEN, 340]

FRANCES 2 [Jonathan 12] b 10 Jan 1765 d 13 Dec 1855 m Hempstead LI 19 Mar 1787 **Duncan Fowler** b LI 18 Jul 1762 d Westbury LI 18 Feb 1852. Ch: Martha 1805 m Jordon Lewis. [Private record, Jeanne Bender, Evansville IN]

FRANCES 3 [Charles 4] b perh Philipstown NY 19 Jun 1802 dsp 27 Nov 1858 m 1) **Beverly Bloomer** m 2) **Elisha C Baxter**. [WRIGHT/FL by Perrine]

FRANCES EMILY 4 [James 16] b 1824.

Frances (Lord) wf [Stephen 5]

FRANCIS 1 of Newtown LI deeded land 21 Sep

1686 "for his natural life" by "loving friend" John Woolston Crafts. [NEWTOWN REC, 342]

FRANCIS 2 of North Castle WestCoNY d by 14 May 1785 m **Anne---**, named adm on his est. [NYCoNY PR in NYHS Vol 38]

FRANCIS GLOW 3 [John 38] b 1812.

FREELOVE 1 [John 9] m **Jonathan Lockwood**. [WRIGHT/FL by Perrine]

FREELOVE 2 [Elijah 1] m 1) (License) 8 Oct 1759 **Samuel Wood** d by 25 Dec 1762 m 2) **Samuel Nichols**. Will of Elijah Wright 1766 names dau Freelove Wood. Issue by Wood (bp St George's Ch, Hempstead): Samuel 1762. [WRIGHT/OB by Perrine; *Dorland Family* (1898), 48; St George's Ch Rec, in RECORD, 11:50; WRIGHT MARR, 52]

FREELOVE 3 m (License) 4 Aug 1761 **Nathan Horton**. [WRIGHT MARR, 52]

FREELOVE 4 [Daniel 16] m **Benjamin Latting** b 7 Jul 1740 d Pleasant Valley NY 22 Jun 1819 son Benjamin & Leah (Simonson) Latting. Of Pleasant Valley NY by 1791. Issue: Deborah 1788, Wright 1791, Benjamin 1794, Sarah 1797, Freelove 1801. ["The Latting Family" by John J Latting, in RECORD (1871), 2:18; WRIGHT/OB by Perrine]

FREELOVE 5 [John 16]. No further record. [DUTCHESS COUNTY HIST, 498]

FREELOVE 6 m by 19 Nov 1805, **Eavon Camron** of Northeast DutCoNY. [Poughkeepsie Journal, 19 Nov 1805]

FREELOVE 7 [Dennis 2]

FREELOVE 7 [Gideon 4]

Freelove (Coles) wf [Caleb 2]
Freelove (Weeks) wf [Joseph 2]

FREEMAN S 1 [William 26]

FROST 1 [Jonathan 12] b 1775 m **Gerry Springsteen**. [Private record, Jeanne Bender, Evansville IN (1979)]

G

GABRIEL 1 b Newtown LI liv 1775 m Fishkill NY (Reformed Ch) 31 Oct 1731 or 25 Jan 1732 **Rebecca Buys** liv 1770 perh dau Abraham Buys. South Ward (Beekman) Dutchess Co NY tax list 1730/1-1735/6. Beekman Tax List 1739/40-Jun 1753. Leased (with sons John & Gabriel Jr) 1 May 1750 Lot 17 (200 a) Beekman Patent. Rebecca wf Gabriel Wright "of Po'keepsie" brot charges against Henry Talerday 1770. He owed 30 pounds to Isaac Smith 1775. Issue: Johannes/John 1733, Samuel 1736, Gabriel Jr. See Samuel 1. [DutCoNY Tax Lists; "Early Leases in the Beekman Patent," by Frank L Doherty, in RECORD (1986), 117:151; DutCoNY Ancient Records #7377 (1770), #9179 (1775)]

GABRIEL 2 [Gabriel 1], b 1730s. With father, leased Beekman Patent Lot 1750. One Gabriel (perh his f) "of Beekman" owed Isaac Vail 1773. "Gabriel Jr" minuteman in Col J Swarthout's Reg't DutCoNY Militia. Perh rec Whitestown, MontCoNY 1790, and Oneida Co NY 1800. ["Early Leases in the Beekman Patent," by Frank L Doherty, in RECORD (1986), 117:151; DutCoNY Court Rec #8620]

GABRIEL 3 [David 6] b 1824.

GEORGE 1 planter of Salem & Braintree, Rehoboth MA, Providence & Newport RI, Gravesend WestCo NY & Flushing LI. Of Gravesend by 1 Mar 1654/5. Of Flushing 27 Dec 1657. Land in Newtown Jan 1663. Deeds land in Rehoboth to son Jonathan of Flushing 2 Feb 1683/4. Issue: Jonathan. ["Captain George Wright", in *Early Rehoboth* by Richard LeBaron Bowen (1948) 3:131-150]

GEORGE 2 "Write" witnessed a deed at Hempstead LI 19 Apr 1689 and another 27 Mar 1699. [NEWTOWN MINUTES, 63, 383]

GEORGE 3 [Jonathan 1] m **Mary---**. Issue (bp Jamaica RDC): James 1705, Jeremias 1716. [WRIGHT/FL by Ferrine]

GEORGE 4 [James of Saybrook CT] b Saybrook CT 2 Sep 1736 d Durham, Green Co NY 15 May 1811 m Saybrook CT 1 Oct 1760 **Anna Lay** b 30 Apr 1741 d 1 Jun 1811. To Durham NY 1788. Region thence called Wrightstreet. Rev War service. Rec Freehold AlbCoNY 1790 w/8 in fam. Issue: George 1761, Anna 1763 m Edmund Bartlett, Temperance 1764 m Phineas Canfield, Caroline 1766 m Daniel Silliman, Lydia 1768 m Eber Cole, Wise 1771, Ambrose 1773, Christopher 1776, James 1778, Benjamin 1780, Phebe 1784 m William Stimpson, Robert Lay 1786 d 1796. [ONE LINE by Cone; 1790 Census]

GEORGE 5 [George 4] b Saybrook CT 31 Mar 1761 d Greenville, Greene Co NY 21 Jul 1821 m 1 Jan 1789 **Elizabeth Post**. Rec Freehold AlbCoNY 1790 w/ 4 in fam. Res Greenville NY. Issue: Asahel 1789, Anson Post 1792, George 1794 d 1797, Lydia 1797 m Walter Barlow, George 1799, Elizabeth 1802 m Jonathan Stokes, Ann 1806 m Joseph R Purington. [ONE LINE by Cone]

GEORGE 6 Beekman NY tax list Jun 1765-1773. [Vincent Wright notes (1979), citing Beekman Tax Lists]

GEORGE 7 [Isaac 2] b Stormville, E Fishkill NY 2 Apr 1805 d Patterson, Putnam Co NY 1 Feb 1875 m 1) perh Philipstown NY ca 1830 **Katherine Nelson** dau Justus & Mary (Odell) Nelson m 2) ca 1840/41 **Mary Susan Davenport** dau John & Mary (Snook) Davenport m 3) perh Cold Spring NY 7 Mar 1844 **Augusta Louise Mead**. Of Cold Spring NY 1842, named in father's will. Issue: Milton H 1834, Hannah E 1837, Nelson 1841, Webster, Mary 1841,

Charles Emerson 1845, Charlotte Louisa 1850+.
[WRIGHT/FL by Perrine; notes by Mary K
Witherbee (1979)]

GEORGE 8 [Adam 1] b 1698.

GEORGE 9 [George 5] b 1799.

GEORGE 10 [John 47]

GEORGE 11 [Isaac 2] b 1805.

GEORGE 12 [Isaac 3]

GEORGE 13 [Simon 1] b 1825.

GEORGE 14 [William 24]

GEORGE T 15 [Gilbert 4] b 1836.

GIDEON 1 [Peter 1] Oyster Bay LI Jun 1685 m **Elizabeth Townsend** dau John & Elizabeth (Montgomerie) Townsend. Exec of his father's estate 1675. She m 2) **Gershom Lockwood**. Issue: Elizabeth m Isaiah Harrison, Peter, Gideon 1675, Anthony, Silvanus, Hannah, John, Tabiatha. [WRIGHT/OB by Perrine]

GIDEON 2 [Gideon 1] b Oyster Bay LI 4 or 8 Jan 1675 d 17 May 1722 ae 47-4-9 m Oyster Bay LI 1702 **Margaret (Urquehart) Shay** d 15 Apr 1720. Will 15 May 1722 proved 28 Aug 1722. Issue: Elizabeth 1702, John 1704/5, Mary 1706, Zebulon 1710, Elijah 1713 [Wright RECORDS by Stark; WRIGHT MARR, 53; WRIGHT/OB by Perrine, 77]

GIDEON 3 [John 5] b 23 Dec 1715 d unm betw 16 Jan/24 Mar 1749/50. Cooper of Oyster Bay. ["Early Ludlam and Related Families," by Clarence A Torrey, in TAG 14:8,9; UNDERHILL GEN, 1:86]

GIDEON 4 [Elijah 1] b 30 Sep 1751 d 12 June 1836 m Smithtown LI 6 Dec 1774 **Mary Dickinson**

by Rev Joshua Hartt (Presby). Issue: Freelove m George Cock, Letitia m Walter Franklin, Susan m Coe Searing, Elizabeth m Obadiah Jackson, Mary m Daniel Cock. ["Marriages of Rev. Joshua Hartt, of Smithtown, L.I." in RECORD, 42:130; WRIGHT/OB by Perrine]

GIDEON 5 [Elijah 1]

GILBERT 1 [Adam 4] yeoman of Oyster Bay, Queens Co NY dsp, will 12 Dec 1783 proved 17 Mar 1784 names mother Elizabeth Wright, sis Almy Wright, Sarah, Deborah, bro Benjamin, William. [NYCoNY PR 36:458 in NYHS 36:269]

GILBERT 2 [Adam 4] of Oyster Bay d Mar 1784 m (License) 17 Nov 1769 **Phebe Jackson.** [WRIGHT/OB by Perrine]

GILBERT 3 m **Nancy---**, who d New Hamburgh NY, 5 Feb 1822. Both mortgaged land in Fishkill to Isaac Sebring 2 Sep 1807. Deeds 3/4 acre in Fishkill to John Dearing 20 Sep 1823. Issue: Jane m John Dearing [DutCoNY Mortg 12:384; DutCoNY Deeds 34:139; POUGHKEEPSIE M&D by Reynolds]

GILBERT 4 b NY ca 1784 liv 1850 Broome, Schoharie Co NY, m **Nancy---** b ca 1791 liv 1850. Carpenter. In their household 1850: Hiram 1826, Eli 1831, George T 1836, Louisa 1841. [1850 Census, Broome, SchoCoNY]

GILBERT 5 [Caleb 4] b Carmel NY 13 Sep 1798 d 28 May 1869 m 1821 **Eliza Wright** b 21 Aug 1802 d 7 May 1892 dau Solomon & Zilpha (Baldwin) Wright. Lived Croton Falls NY. See his will PutnCoNY PR #1830, B:13. Issue: Elizabeth 1822, Green 1824, David 1826, Jackson 1828, Susan 1830, Zilpha 1832, Mary Ann 1834, Simon 1836, Theodore 1838, Theda 1840, Amanda 1843. [WRIGHT/OB by Perrine, 194]

GLORIANA 1 [Daniel 4] b 1774 dsp 1789. [WestCoNY PR A:152; WRIGHT/FL by Perrine]

GRACE 1 [Samuel 1] bp Newtown (Presby Ch) LI 8 Jan 1738 (with sister Deborah [qv] perh same who m Newtown (Presby Ch) LI 15 Mar 1739 **Obadiah Smith** of Jamaica LI. [WRIGHT/FL by Perrine; Newtown Presby Ch Rec]

GREEN 1 [Caleb 4]

GREEN 2 [Gilbert 5] b 1824.

GRIETJE 1 [Henry 2] bp Fishkill RDC 29 Apr 1733 (sponsor Gabriel Rydt). [Fishkill RDC Rec]

GROSBECK 1 [John 36]

H

HAIGHT 1 [Charles 4] b prob Fishkill NY 24 Dec 1787 d Mar 1789. [WRIGHT/FL by Perrine]

HALLETT 1 [Joseph 5] d by 23 Oct 1784, named in father's will. Issue (from will of Joseph): James. [NYCoNY PR 19:384, in NYHS 29:99]

HAMILTON MERCER 1 [Isaac 2] b 1808.

HAMILTON MERCER 2 [Isaac 6] b 1833.

HANNAH 1 [Job 1] m **Robert Townsend**. [WRIGHT/OB by Perrine]

HANNAH 2 [John 6] b perh Huntington LI 24 Feb 1731. [WRIGHT RECORDS by Stark]

HANNAH 3 [John 2] prob b Flushing LI m Aug 1732 **Joseph Haight** of Rye NY b 1712. Res Brinckerhoffville NY. Taxed Highland of DutCoNY 1772. Issue: Daniel 1732/33, William, Esther, Phebe m Col Zebulon Butler, Mary 1739/40 m Justus Nelson, John 1741, Joseph of NYC, Martha m 1) John McKeel m 2) ---Baxter, Sylvanus, Stephen, Beverly, Hannah. [WRIGHT/FL by Perrine; SCJ]

HANNAH 4 [Daniel 3]. No further record. [WRIGHT/FL by Perrine]

HANNAH 5 [Reuben 2]. No further record. [WRIGHT/FL by Perrine]

HANNAH 6 [David 5] m **David Vance**. [DAR Lineage Book 119:59]

HANNAH 7 m (License) 4 May 1758 **Daniel Barnes.** [WRIGHT MARR, 53]

HANNAH 8 [Jonathan 5] m DutCoNY 1) 28 Oct 176? **Moses Drake** m 2) after 1802 **Thomas Hunt** of Hunt's Point LI, widower of her sis Melicent [qv]. [NY MARR; *Andrew Ward and His Descendants* by Geo K Warde (1910), 612; WRIGHT MARR, 53]

HANNAH 9 [Samuel 3] b 14 Oct 1790 bp Flushing (St George's Ch) LI 29 Aug 1795. [St George's Ch Rec. in RECORD, 112:42]

HANNAH 10 [Dennis 2]

HANNAH 11 [Ephraim 1] b 1731.

HANNAH 12 [Daniel 3]

HANNAH 13 [Gideon 1]

HANNAH 14 [John 36] b 1791.

HANNAH 15 [John 46] b 1807.

HANNAH 16 [Enos 1] b 1813.

HANNAH MARIA 17 [Isaac 3]

Hannah (Hart) wf [Joseph 19]
Hannah (Thurston) wf [David 1]
Hannah (Wood) wf [Ephraim 1]

HARRIET 1 [Samuel 13] b 1797.

HARRIET 2 [Wise 2] b 1809.

HARRISON 1 [William 13]

HARRISON 2 [Jacob 11] b 1846.

HARVEY See also JAMES HARVEY.

HARVEY 1 [John 16]. No further record. [DUTCHESS COUNTY HIST, 498]

HARVEY H 2 [Jacob 11]

HELEN 1 sis of [James 9].

HENRIETTA M 1 [Abraham 6]

HENRIETTA 2 [Wise 2] b 1837.

HENRY 1 [Jonathan 1] d Flushing LI ca 1715 m by 1698 **Mary---**. Will 8 Dec 1713 proved 21 Dec 1715 exec Thomas Ford, Anthony Gleanee. Issue (from 1698 Census and will): Sarah, Abigail, Hannah m by 1713, Mary. [NYCoNY PR 8:432 in NYHS 26:159; WRIGHT/FL by Perrine]

HENRY 2 aka Hendricus Rydt of Fishkill NY m perh Port Richmond SI by 1728 **Aaltje Marling/Marlyn**. South Ward (Beekman) Tax List 1730/1-1736/7. Perh same in Jacob Swarthout's DutCoNY Militia 1760 & Capt Terbush's Co 1761. Issue (bp Port Richmond RDC & Fishkill RDC): Henricus/Henry 1728/9, Elizabeth 1731, Grietje 1733 (Gabriel Rydt spons at her bp). See HENRY 3. [Fishkill RDC Rec; Beekman Tax Lists; DUTCHESS COUNTY HIST, 88,89]

HENDRICK 3 [Anthony 2] b by 1718. Of Staten Island. Co-exec 1746 of father's 1739 will. See HENRY 2.

HENRY 4 [Henry 2] bp Port Richmond (RDC) Staten Is NY 1728/29 (witn Borent Martline & Dina V.Name). [Fort Richmond RDC Rec]

HENRY 5 b Staten Is NY ca 1733. Swarthout's Company DutCoNY Militia 1760 (age 27 farmer), Capt Isaac Terbush's DutCoNY Militia 1761 (age 27 laborer). ["NY Muster Rolls 1755-1764" in NYHS Vol 24 (1891)]

HENRY 6 [John 47]

HENRY A 7 [Richard 2] b 1827.

HENRY NELSON 8 [John 38] b 1813.

HEPSIBER 1 [Matthew 1]

Hester/Hetty (Colwell) wf [Isaac 6]

HETTY M 1 [Jacob 11]

HEZEKIAH 1 [Anthony 2] b prob Staten Island NY 1715 d 1774 m **Christian Slaght** dau Barent Slaght of Staten Is. He named in father's 1739 will. Will of Barent Slaght (Staten Island Oct 1772) names dau "Christian wife of Hezekiah Wright, Esq." and Hezekiah was a witn. No chr found. One Hezekiah, Joshua, Anthony Wright witn to will of Wynant Winans 1732/3. Property on SI mentioned in bro Anthony's 1761 will. See ANTHONY 4. [NYCoNY PR in NYHS 29:50 (Slaght), 33:158- 159 (Winans); Worcester Co MD PR 31:469 (Anthony Wright); WRIGHT/OB by Perrine]

HIRAM 1 m New Lebanon NY 24 Nov 1825 **Sophia Platt.** [WRIGHT MARR, 54]

HIRAM 2 of Po'keepsie NY m **Joanna---**, and had partial issue: Sarah (d 3 Oct 1849 ae 22-3-25. [VRs from Poughkeepsie newspaper dated 10 Oct 1849, reported by Clifford M. Buck, Salt Point NY]

HIRAM 3 [Abel 1]

HIRAM 4 [Robert 4]

HIRAM 5 [Gilbert 4] b 1826.

HORATIO 1 [Daniel 16] aka Horace (per Perrine) dsp m 18 Nov 1782 **Mary Underhill** dau Joseph Underhill. [UNDERHILL GEN, 138; WRIGHT/OB by Perrine]

HORATIO NELSON 2 [Abel 1]

Huyla (Vanduerson) wf [John 17]

I

IRA 1 [William 14]

ISAAC 1 [John 2] prob m Hempstead (St George Episc Ch) LI 23 Jun 1736 **Ruth Lee.** Issue: Ruth m ----Lee, Robert 1737, John. [WRIGHT/FL by Perrine; WRIGHT MARR, 54]

ISAAC R 2 [Robert 1] b Somers NY 1764 d E Fishkill NY 4 Mar 1842, m Bedford NY 1787 (1785 per "Wright Marriages") **Mary Hamilton** d E Fishkill NY 14 Sep 1849 ae 85-9-19 dau Mercer Belden. Mortgaged in Fishkill 1817. Issue (from will): Daniel I 1791, Charlotte m ----Samuel Colwell, Benjamin Belden 1793, Elizabeth, Isaac D 1797, James L 1795, George 1805, Hamilton Mercer 1808, William 1809, Abraham 1812, Sarah m Danial Doane, Mary m Nathaniel Perry. [DutCoNY PR #3778; DutCoNY Mortg 23:245; WRIGHT/FL by Perrine; DUTCHESS COUNTY HIST. 235; WRIGHT MARR, 54]

ISAAC I 3 [John 16] b ca 1789, d 4 Feb 1871 (obit 9 Mar 1871) ae 82 m Fishkill NY **Janet Howe**, named in 1826 mortgage. Of Fishkill NY 1826, to Stanford NY 1836, of Beekman NY 1842, named in father's will. Issue (from his bio): Margaret, Hannah Maria, Ymar, James Harvey 1820, John, Lucy Ann m Clark Guernsey, Phebe m Eli Wright, George (of Mount Ross, Milan NY). [DutCoNY Mortg 33:401; VR's from Poughkeepsie newspapers, reported by Clifford M. Buck, Salt Point NY; DUTCHESS COUNTY HIST, 498]

ISAAC 4 [Jonathan 12] b prob Hempstead LI 1784 m 1) **Amelia Baker** m 2) **Mercy Ann Horton.**

Issue: Elizabeth 1811 m John Bailey, Angeline 1812 m ---Von Vorhus, Thomas 1812 (twin), Marvin 1816, Robert 1818, Susanna 1828, John 1834, Jordon F 1837. [Private record, Jeanne Bender (1979) citing Family Bible of Isaac Wright]

ISAAC 5 [Charles 4] b 30 Sep 1790 bp Fishkill (RDC) NY 28 Nov 1790 d 4 Apr 1881 ae 91 m **Phebe Warren** d 19 May 1835 ae 31 bur Cold Spring NY dau Samuel & Ann (Hustis) Warren. Res Cold Spring NY. Issue: 3 chn, all d young. [WRIGHT/FL by Perrine; PUTNAM COUNTY by Pelletreau, 573]

ISAAC 6 [Isaac 2] b 21 Jun 1797 d 22 Aug 1865 or 1866 ae 68 bur LaGrangeville NY m 1819 **Hetty Colwell** d 23 Aug 1877 ae 77 dau Samuel & Polly (Smith) Colwell sis of Samuel Colwell who m Charlotte Wright (dau Isaac of Fishkill). Farmer Fishkill NY proprietor of general store Cold Spring NY. Issue: Charles 1820, William 1828, Elizabeth 1836, Hamilton Mercer 1833. [WRIGHT/FL by Perrine]

ISAAC 7 [Daniel 13] twin b prob Berne, Albany Co NY 29 Aug 1804 d Orfordville, Rock Co WI 1 Apr 1891 m Oxford, Chenango Co NY ca 1831 **Sally Williams** b 6 Jun 1809 d Orfordville WI 27 Aug 1864 dau Eber & Martha (Bennett) Williams. Issue: William dy, Mary C, Edmund L 1834, Minnie. [Private rec of Mary K Witherbee, Oneonta NY (1979); Family Group Sheet by Ellen L Nelson, Fairbanks AK, in *Wright Book of Family Ancestry Sheets, Vol 1* by Claudette Maerz, Bloomington IN]

ISAAC R 8 [Robert 4] d Fairfax VA by Dec 1851 m **Phebe---**. Family mentioned in father's will. Issue: Martha, Phebe Ann. [DutCoNY PR (Robert Wright) #2323]

ISAAC 9 [William 23]

ISAAC CANDEE 10 [Charles 5]

ISAAC D 11 [Isaac 2] b 1797.

Isabel (---) wf [William 24]

J

JACKSON 1 [Gilbert 5] b 1828.

JACOB 1 [Job 1] d Chester Co PA 1735 m 1) **Hannah Townsend** m 2) 1728 **Mary Richardson**. Finally settled in Whiteland, Chester Co PA. Wid Mary renounced adm 28 May 1735. Issue: Susannah, Abigail, Keziah m Samuel Frost b 1706. [FROST GEN, 27; WRIGHT/OB by Perrine]

JACOB 2 [John 2] b LI 1721 perh d 1777 m prob Stephentown NY **Elizabeth Haight** d Somers NY bur Somers (Crompond Second Presby Ch Cem) dau John Haight. Purchaser in Cortlandt pct with bro Daniel 22 May 1762. Estate on Fishkill tax list 1777. Capt at time of marriage. Perh of Crum Elbow 1749-1752. Issue: Sarah 1747 m Thomas Nelson, Jacob (d in Rev), Nathan/Nathaniel, Joseph (d in Rev), Elizabeth m Seth Whitney, Letitia m Robert Lane, Simeon. [WRIGHT/FL by Perrine; *Thomas Davenport...and His Descendants* by Dorothy Giles and Irma Franklin, 211; *Richard Washburn Family Genealogy* by Ada C. Haight, 178]

JACOB 3 [Edmund 1] aka Jacob Ryt m **Antje/Anna Rol/Ral/Roe**. Issue (bp Staten Is (Port Richmond RDC) NY: Maria 1722, Susanna 1727. [Port Richmond RDC Rec; WRIGHT/OB by Perrine]

JACOB 4 [Daniel 2] b LI 12 Jan 1747/8 d Trenton NJ Oct 1807 m **Ann Vandergrift** b Burlington NJ 12 Sep 1753. Rev War soldier. [Query 3973-9 *Connecticut Nutmegger* 10:278]

JACOB 5 [Edmund 2] m (License) 16 Dec 1736 **Catherine Pell**. [WRIGHT/OB by Perrine; WRIGHT

MARR, 54]

JACOB 6 Northeast NY tax list Jun 1760--1769. Also Jacob "Right" on Nine Partners, Crum Elbow, Charlotte Tax List Jun 1748 - Feb 1760. [CRUM ELBOW TAX LISTS]

JACOB 7 b say 1735 m **Mary**---. At Rumbout 14 Jun 1762 when Jacob and chn Lydia, Elizabeth, William F, Joseph H were bp into St George's Ch Hempstead. Perh same "of Rombout Pct" who refused to sign the Association Aug 1775. Issue: Lydia, Elizabeth, William F, Joseph H. [St George's Ch Rec in RECORD (1884), 11:49; "Rombout Precinct Loyalists," in RECORD, 112:14]

JACOB 8 [Joseph 12] b 21 Apr 1790 bp Fishkill (Reformed Ch) 26 Jun 1790, living 1809 (per gf will). [Fishkill Reformed Ch Rec; DutCoNY PR D:125]

JACOB 9 of Clinton, Dutchess Co NY 1800, aged 26/44 with "wife", 2 m under 10, 2 f under 10. [1800 Census]

JACOB 10 of Cobleskill NY m **Catherine**---. Issue (bp Zion Evangel Ch): Thomas 1810. [IGI 84]

JACOB 11 of Berne NY, b ca 1799 d Berne NY 1867 m **Amanda**---, and bo't 80 a of Johannes TenEyck farm (Lot 477) Berne 7 May 1834, sold 70 a of it to David Wright 9 Mar 1843. Rec Berne 1850. Adm 15 Feb 1866. Heirs quitclaimed 27 Mar 1867. Issue: Alanson, Julia Ann, Nancy E, Sally m ---Pinckney, Alfred, Hetty M m Adam Waggoner, Harvey H, Ellen A m ---Gardner, Margaret, Harrison, Erwin, Laura. [AlbCoNY Deeds 207:307, AlbCoNY PR 11:7,72]

JACOB 12 of Poughkeepsie NY m **Elizabeth**---. Both mortg land in Po'keepsie 1842-1843. [DutCoNY Mortg 73:132, 74:276,453]

JACOB 13 yeoman of Flushing, Queens Co NY, adm 9 Jul 1784 to bro Jonathan of Fredericksburgh Pct, tavernkeeper. [NYCoNY Adm in NYHS 36:412]

JACOB 14 [Job 4] b 1753 d DutCoNY 12 or 13 Dec 1833 m 2) **Mary Griffin**. 1776 commanded Col John Lasher's Continental NY Regt. Member Soc of the Cincinnati. On Invalid Pension roll (pvt in Boyle's US Art'y) from 17 May 1816 at $95 per annum. Issue: Julia Ann m Archibald Lamont. [DAR Patriot Index; DAR Lineage Bk 9:298; WRIGHT/OB by Perrine; NY PENSION ROLL (1835)]

JACOB 15 d 1811. Capt in Rev with NY service. On list of invalid pensioners whose location was lost due to distruction of records in 1814 War. [NY PENSION ROLL (1835)]

JACOB 16 [Jacob 2] killed ae 21 in Rev by British light horseman "whilst on a visit to a young lady in the lower part of Westchester County". [Ada C. Haight's *Richard Hashburn Family Genealogy*, by Ada C Haight, 178]

JACOB 17 m (License) 30 Oct 1777 **Rebecca McDonnell**. [WRIGHT MARR, 54]

JACOB 18 [Joshua 2] b 1831.

JACOB 19 [Robert 4]. Of Fairfax VA.

JAMES 1 [George 2] bp Jamaica (RDC) NY 18 Oct 1705.

JAMES 2 of WestCoNY, b England ca 1741. Enlisted in Capt Jonathan Ogden's WestCoNY Militia 17 Apr 1758 (aged 17). [NY Muster Rolls, in NYHS Vol 24]

JAMES 3 m Conn ca 1772/6 **Elizabeth Lee** (relative of Gen Charles Lee). Later of Schoharie Co NY. [Query 6978 by E.J.B in

Transcript 17 Feb 1904]

JAMES 4 [Adam 3] b 14 Mar 1721 d Bedford NY 17 May 1776 m 1 Jan 1756 **Almy/Amy Patterson** d 11 May 1803 bur Newcastle (St George's Episc) NY. Of Bedford, New Purchase WestCoNY. Will 3 Jun 1775 proved 20 May 1776 names wf, son, 5 daus. Issue: Sarah 1757 m Thomas Hawxhurst, Jesse, Mary 1761 m Jesse Simons, Amy m Jacob Conklin, Phebe m Benjamin Harice, Fanny. Perh the "James Wright dec'd" whose former homestead mortg 5 Jun 1789 by Walter Seaman. [NYCoNY PR 33:418 in NYHS 33:303; WestCoNY Mortg D:252; WRIGHT/OB by Perrine]

JAMES 5 [Daniel 3] m 17 Dec 1786 **Elizabeth Bailey**. Acct with Dr Cornelius 20 May 1789 to 31 Dec 1803 identifies him as "brother of Micajah." [WRIGHT/FL by Perrine; CORNELIUS LEDGER]

JAMES 6 of Franklin, DutCoNY Oct 1798, when dwellinghouse listed (6th subdivision). See JAMES 8. [PUTNAM COUNTY HIST by Pelletreau, 636]

JAMES JR 7 perh the "James" who m Bangall DutCoNY 24 May 1790 **Betsey Hammond**. Perh "James Jr" rec Washington DutCoNY 1790 w/3 in fam. Perh same of Northeast DutCoNY who mortg 8 Feb 1803 to Isaac Smith of Little Nine Partners (Lot 36 in Nine Partners). [WRIGHT MARR, 54; 1790 Census; DutCoNY Mortg 9:305]

JAMES 8 of Oyster Bay NY, m **Betsey---**, and deed land in Franklin to Alexander Kidd, 17 Nov. 1799. See JAMES 6. [DutCoNY Deeds 16:153-155]

JAMES 9 of NYC, adm 13 May 1784 to James Howman of Horseneck CT. Issue (from will): James ("natural son" by Ann Ellsworth of NYC - land in Argyle AlbCoNY). Also names sis Jane wf John Pock, sis Helen, uncle Hugh Atchison.

[NYCoNY PR in NYHS]

JAMES 10 [James 9] liv 13 May 1784, bequeathed interest by his father in a lot in Argyle, Albany Co NY.

JAMES 11 [William 3] b prob North Castle WestCoNY 1787 d 1871 m **Cynthia Clarke** b 1794 d 1851. [DAR Lineage Book 118:175]

JAMES 12 [Abraham 2] living 1791, named in will of gf Abraham Wright. Perhaps "James the sadler" who had an acct with Dr Cornelius 4 Mar 1796 to 1802. [WRIGHT/FL by Perrine; CORNELIUS LEDGER]

JAMES 13 [Charles 4] b prob Fishkill NY 31 Jul 1792 dsp 28 Aug 1817. [WRIGHT/FL by Perrine]

JAMES 14 [Micaijah 1] b 2 Jan 1799 dsp 21 Aug 1864. Res Oswichee AL. [WRIGHT/FL by Perrine]

JAMES 15 m Carmel NY ca 18 Nov 1801 **Sarah Hall**. [POUGHKEEPSIE M&D by Reynolds]

JAMES 16 [Isaac 2] b 11 Aug 1796 d New Orleans LA 9 Oct 1854 bur Pass Christian, Mississippi m perh Beekman NY 14 Nov 1818 **Martha Denton** d 22 Nov 1884 bur Cold Spring NY dau Solomon & Clarissa Anderson (Fowler) Denton. Both quit claim (with other Dentons) Solomon Denton farm in Beekman 1829. Issue: Abram James 1822, Frances Emily 1824, Jane 1826. [WRIGHT/FL by Perrine; notes by Mary K Witherbee (1979); DutCoNY Deeds 43:190]

JAMES 17 [Simon 1] b Cortlandt NY 26 May 1802 m 1) 27 Jan 1824 **Zilla Hart** dau Samuel & Hannah (Garrison) Hart m 2) 17 Aug 1862 **Mariel (Hathaway) Miles** wid of Jonathan Miles of Woodhull NY. [SCJ, 352]

JAMES 18 WestCoNY m 29 Oct 1807 **Sarah Hull**. [SCJ, 383]

JAMES 19 [William 3] b 1787.

JAMES J 20 [Samuel 10] b 21 Jun 1787 d prob Middleburg, Schoharie Co NY 15 Aug 1857 bur Cotton Hill Cem m **Christina Scott**. Farmer of Middleburgh 1850. Issue (from Census): Lucretia, Richard J, Abram, Samuel J, Dorcas ca 1822. [1850 Census; Private record, Joseph V Wright, Haverford PA (1977)]

JAMES L 21 [Isaac 2] m Vicksburg MS **Lucy White**. Of New Orleans LA 1842, named in father's will. [WRIGHT/FL by Perrine]

JAMES 22 [Ambrose 1]

JAMES 23 [George 4]b 1778

JAMES 24 [Hallett 1]

JAMES 25 [Jonas 1]

JAMES 26 [William 13] b 1814.

JAMES HARVEY 27 b ca 1804, d Po'keepsie NY, 31 Nov 1848 ae 44. [POUGHKEEPSIE M&D by Reynolds; CEM INSC by Frost]

JAMES HARVEY 28 [Isaac 3] b 1820.

JAMES HARVEY 29 [David 10] b 1824.

JAMES HARVEY 30 [Abraham 7] b 1831.

JAMES L 31 [Isaac 2] b 1795.

JANE 1 m (License) 12 Mar 1765 **Thomas Skidmore**. [WRIGHT MARR, 54]

JANE 2 [Andrew 1] b by 1747.

JANE 3 [Gilbert 3] m Dutchess Co NY, 6 Jan 1814 **John Dearing** of Fishkill. [POUGHKEEPSIE M&D by Reynolds]

JANE 4 [William 4] 9 Jan 1794 bp Flushing (St George's Ch) LI 5 29 Aug 1798 perh m Flushing LI 25 May 1811 **Ananias Langdon**. [St George's Ch Rec in RECORD, 110:2, 112:42]

JANE BELL 5 [William 4] bp Flushing (St George's Ch) LI 5 May 1810 m Flushing (St George's Ch) 26 Feb 1835 **John J Jones**, both then of NYC. But see JANE 1794, above. [St George's Ch Rec, in RECORD]

JANE 6 [James 16] b 1826.

JANE 7 [John 35]

JANE 8 [Gilbert 3]

JANE ELIZA 9 [Abraham 7]

Jane (Allen) wf [Abraham 7]
Jane (Blain) wf [William 14]
Jane (Gregg) wf [Benjamin 7]
Jane (Hughart) wf [Peter 6]
Jane (Sayre) wf [Obadiah 1]
Janet (Howe) wf [Isaac 3]
JASON 1 [Joseph 16] b 1821.

JEAN 1 m Richmond LI 25 Apr 1755 **Samuel Denike**. [WRIGHT MARR, 54]

JEANETTE 1 [Cruger 1] b 1808.

JEMIMA 1 m **Richard Horton** b White Plains NY 1721 son John & Elizabeth (Lee) Horton. Res Peekskill NY. Issue: Elijah 1739, George, William, Richard. [HORTON GEN, 7]

JEMIMA 2 [Charles 4] b 1806.

JEMIMA JANE 3 [Jesse 1]

Jemima (Haight) wf [William 1]

JENNY 1 [John 30] bp Rumbout (Presby Ch) 15

Feb. 1767 (with sis Rachel). [Rumbout Presby Ch Rec]

JEREMIAS 1 [George 2] bp Jamaica (RDC) NY 8 Jul 1716. [WRIGHT/FL by Perrine]

JERUSHA 1 [Daniel 6]

JERVIS 1 [Joseph 16] b 1821.

JESSE 1 [James 4] d QueCoNY 1816 m Fishkill NY ca 7 June 1803 **Magdelen Kipp** of Fishkill. Issue: Jemima Jane. [POUGHKEEPSIE M&D by Reynolds; WRIGHT/OB by Perrine]

JESSE B 2 m 20 Feb 1811 **Margaret Bennet** bp Oyster Bay 14 Apr 1790 dau Nicholas & Maria (Duryea) Bennet. ["Willem Adriaense Bennet of Brooklyn," in RECORD (1963), 94:164]

Joanna (---) wf [Hiram 2]

JOB 1 [Peter 1] b 1636 d Oyster Bay 13 Sep 1706 m **Rachel Townsend** dau John & Susannah (Harcourt) Townsend. Will 6 Sept 1706. Issue: Anthony, Keziah m John Burr, Rachel 1689 m Thomas Stokes, Hannah, Jacob, Elizabeth. [FROST GEN, 27; WRIGHT/OB by Perrine]

JOB 2 [Adam 1] Of Oyster Bay LI.

JOB 3 [Jonathan 1] perh m **Mary Leverich** dau Caleb Leverich of Newtown LI. Inherited homestead with bros Charles & John. Prob witn will of Thomas Ellison of Hempstead 1697/8 and of Henry Franklin of Flushing 1702. Land in Newtown NY mentioned in will of Joseph Sackett 1719. Issue: prob Leverich say 1710/20, perh John. [WRIGHT/FL by Perrine; Query 943, by Thomas V Leverich, in RECORD, 109:28,]

JOB 4 m 1734 (int rec Purchase Meeting 13 4th Month & 11 5th Month 1734) **Ursula Carpenter**. Quaker. Issue: Rachel m Samuel Carpenter,

Elizabeth m Jacob Weeks, Jacob, Job. [WRIGHT/OB by Perrine; Purchase Monthly Meeting Rec; *Carpenter Family* (1901), 106]

JOB 5 of Cortland Manor WestCoNY d 1771. Will 3 Jul 1771 proved 10 Aug 1771 names exec Robert Weeks. [NYCoNY PR 28:64 in NYHS 41:442]

JOB 6 [Job 4] d Cortlandt WestCoNY ca 1784 m 1) 10 Sep 1732 **Phebe Yeomans** of Oyster Bay m 2) **Sarah---**. Will 4 5th Mo 1783 proved 10 Mar 1784. Issue (from will): William (eldest), Job, Rachel, Marythe, Phebe, Sarah. Also perh Benjamin (by 1st wf, per Perrine). [NYCoNY PR 36:317 in NYHS 36:211; WRIGHT/OB by Perrine]

JOB 7 Nine Partners tax list Jun 1768-Jun 1769. [CRUM ELBOW TAX LISTS, 44]

JOB 8 [Job 6] living 1783, to inherit bulk of father's estate. [WRIGHT/OB by Perrine, which advises see Bolton's *History of the County of Westchester*, 2:529]

JOB 9 deeds 10 Apr 1790, 136 acres in Saratoga Patent [Lots 39 & 46 E bank of Hudson], to Abraham Wright. [AlbCoNY Deeds 13:326]

JOB 10 [Joseph 1] d 1784. Of Westbury LI. [WRIGHT/OB by Perrine]

JOEL 1 [David 5] perh of New Windsor NY. [DAR Lineage Book 119:59]

JOEL 2 [Benjamin 4] b prob Somers NY 12 Dec 1793 d 3 Apr 1875. [WRIGHT/FL by Perrine]

JOHANNA 1 [Robert 1] m **Edward Vermilyea**. [WRIGHT/FL by Perrine]

JOHANNA 2 [William 13]

JOHN 1 [Nicholas 2] b prob Lynn MA ca 1635 d Oyster Bay LI 1707 m Oyster Bay LI **Mary**

Townsend dau Henry & Ann (Cole) Townsend. Builder. Issue: Rose m 1) Nathaniel Coles 2) John Townsend, Eliphal m Henry Townsend, Mary. [*Winthrop-Babcock Genealogy* by J.L. Frost, 572]

JOHN 2 [Jonathan 1] b prob Flushing LI ca 1680 m after 1698 **Sarah---**. Known as John Wright of Yorktown, WestCoNY. Said to have d 1768 leaving estate to kin Eleanor Winstanly & chn. See JOHN 3. Issue: Abraham 1708, Sarah m ----Lee, Hannah m Joseph Haight, Isaac, Jonathan, Jacob 1721, John 1710/20, Daniel 1708/18. [WRIGHT/FL by Perrine]

JOHN 3 watchmaker of Flushing LI & Liverpool Eng d Flushing LI 1768. Will "of Flushing" 8 Mar 1768 proved 15 Apr 1768 in NY. Bequests to Eleanor Winstanly wid of William Winstanly schoolmaster (late of Liverpool Eng) and her sons William & Edward and daus (not named). Also to Cronton School, Lancashire (for books & educ of poor). To nephew [? John Winstanly] (eldest son of William Winstanly Jr) land in Penny Lane, Cronton (else to nephew's bro William), nephew's sis Nelly. Remainder to John Winstanly and his chn. Exec bro/law Peter Pemberton, "friends in NY" James Bavelot of NY, **Jonathan Wright** & John Field Jr of Flushing. 1 guinea to nephew Edward Baily shipwright. Will of John Wright "of Liverpool, but at his death of the Island of Nassau, province of New York" filed Chester Eng 1771. Adm of William Winstanley schoolmaster of Liverpool, 1765. [NYCoNY FR 26:213 in NYHS 31:147; *Wills in Probate Registry, Chester, 1761-1780*. Record Society for the Publication of Original Documents Relating to Lancashire and Cheshire. (1898-9) 38:109]

JOHN 4 [? Job 1] perh b Newtown LI. [WRIGHT/FL by Perrine]

JOHN 5 [Gideon 1] d prob Oyster Bay 1737 m 1) 27 Jan 1707/8 **Abigail Barker** d by 9 Nov 1722 m 2) **Sarah Ludlam** b 1689 d by 1729 dau Joseph & Elizabeth (Townsend) Ludlam. Issue: Abigail 1712/3 m John Feekes, Gideon 1715, John, Elizabeth m Edmond Weeks. ["Early Ludlam and Related Families," by Clarence A Torrey in TAG 14:8; WRIGHT/OB by Perrine]

JOHN 6 [Gideon 2] b Oyster Bay LI 14 Jan 1704 m Huntington LI (1st Ch) 26 Dec 1729 **Ruth Bailey**. Issue: Hannah 1731, Amelia 1734, John Jr 1736, Augustine 1740, William 1744, Zebulon 1747, Ruth 1751. [WRIGHT RECORDS by Stark; First Ch Huntington LI Rec, 64]

JOHN 7 weaver of WestCoNY, b LI ca 1711. In Capt Johnathan Ogdens WestCo Militia 22 Aug 1758 (age 47). [NY Muster Rolls in NYHS Vol 24]

JOHN 8 shoemaker, b Queens Co NY ca 1718. Enlisted in Capt Richard Hulet's QueCo Militia 4 Apr 1758 (age 40). [NY Muster Rolls in NYHS Vol 24]

JOHN 9 [John 2] b prob Flushing LI ca 1710/20 d Stamford CT 1770 m 1) **Sarah---** m 2) by 18 Sep 1739 **Sarah---**. Of WestCoNY, later to Stamford CT. Will 10 Oct 1769 proved 3 Apr 1770. Issue: William 1736, Daniel, Freelove m Jonathan Lockwood, Philena m ---Warner/Waring, Sarah m ---Styat?, James 1739, Reuben, Rachel m ---Simpkins, Elizabeth, Prudence, Amy. [WRIGHT/FL by Perrine, citing Stamford CT PR]

JOHN 10 [Ephraim 1] b Lebanon CT 18 Mar 1726. No further record. [ABEL WRIGHT by Stephen Wright, in REGISTER (1881)]

JOHN 11 [Gabriel 1] bp Fishkill (RDC) NY 4 Feb 1733 (spons Hannes & Elizabet Buys). With father & bro Gabriel leased Lot Beekman Patent 1750. Beekman Tax List Feb-Jun 1756. [Fishkill

RDC Rec; "Early Leases in the Beekman Patent," by Frank L Doherty, in RECORD (1986), 117:151]

JOHN 12 cordwainer of Ulster Co NY, b Ireland ca 1734. Enlisted 29 Mar 1760 in Capt Clinton's UlsCo Militia. NY Muster Rolls in NYHS Vol 24]

JOHN 13 [John 6] b perh Oyster Bay LI 25 Dec 1736 m **Elizabeth Carpenter** b 2 May 1746 dau Ephraim & Hannah (Canfield) Carpenter. Res Kent NY. Issue (from Gideon Wright's Acct Bk): Ephraim 1766, Amelia 1767, Samuel 1768, Hannah 1771, Elizabeth 1772, John 1775, Rachel 1777, Mary 1777 (twin), Ruth 1779. [WRIGHT RECORDS by Stark]

JOHN 15 [William 5] b Oyster Bay 27 Mar 1707 d Oyster Bay 12 Jan 1750 m (License) Suckscally Wigwam LI 15 Apr 1736 **Serviah/Zeraiah Wright** dau Edmund & Sarah (Townsend) Wright. Will 8 Jan 1749/50 proved 27 Mar 1749/50. Issue (from will): John 1737 (eldest son in will), William 1738 dy, Elizabeth, Nicholas, Anne m 1) Robert Cookes 2) Joshua Hammond, William (2nd) 1748. [NYCoNY PR 17:83 in NYHS 28:260; WRIGHT/OB by Perrine; WRIGHT MARR, 54]

JOHN 16 [Isaac 1] farmer, "native" of Fishkill. Perh rec Fishkill DutCoNY 1790 w/7 in fam. Perh same "John of Fishkill" who had acct with Dr Cornelius 15 Nov 1797 to 26 Jan 1801 naming "wf," mentioned also in acct of Peter Maybee. Issue: Polly, Susan, Lydia, Ruth, Isaac I ca 1789, John, Aaron, Esther, Dena, Peter, Freelove, Harvey. [DUTCHESS COUNTY HIST, 498; WRIGHT/FL by Perrine, who lists only Isaac and Peter as chn; 1790 Census; CORNELIUS LEDGER]

JOHN 17 of NYC [Jonas 1] d NYC by 1762 m NY State Records 16 Dec 1752 **Huyla Vanduerson**. His chn named in will of their gf Jonas Wright. She prob m 2) NYC (state license) 8

Jul 1762 **Austin Reynolds**. Issue (bp NY Presby Ch): John Foret 1753, Catlen/Catherine 1755. [NY MARR, 54-55; 1st & 2nd Presby Ch Rec in RECORD, Vol 4.]

JOHN 18 [? Job 1] assessor North Castle NY 3 Apr 1753. Possible issue: William 1753. [suggested by Dorothea White, citing *Historic Documents of North Castle* (1975)]

JOHN 19 [David 3] b perh Hempstead NY ca 1753 d New Windsor, Orange Co NY, 21 Sept 1838 ae 86 m **Abigail**--- b ca 1757 d 14 Dec 1827 ae 69. Acc to tombstone, served in a DutCoNY Militia commanded by Col Jacobus Swartwout. Also said in 5th Ulster Co Militia. Res New Windsor, Orange Co NY. Will 30 Jan 1813. Perh rec New Windsor UlstCoNY 1790 w/5 in fam. Issue: William J, John, Mary m ---Preston. [OraCoNY PR K;231; WRIGHTS OF LONG ISLAND by Francis Wright; 1790 Census]

JOHN 20 m (License) 19 May 1757 **Elizabeth Sellars**. [NY MARR, 55]

JOHN 21 d NYC by 1 Jul 1775 m prob NYC (license) 9 Nov 1757 **Jane Montanye** dau Thomas & Rebecca Montanye whose 1774 will names Jane wf John Wright. Adm on his est 1 Jul 1775 to moth/law Rebecca Montanye. [NY MARR; NYCoNY Adm in NYHS 32:374; 400 YEARS by Larry Wright, 225, which says he had Rev War service and d 1824]

JOHN 22 b say 1755 d prob Albany Co NY by 1820 m Rhinebeck (RDC) 13 Nov 1776 **Mary Barton**. Bo't Lot 501 Rensselaerwyck Manor, Berne NY. Perh "John Jr" rec Clinton DutCoNY 1790 w/7 in fam. Rec Berne AlbCoNY 1800. Issue: Elisha ca 1778, Susannah 1782, William J ca 1792, Joseph 1795, Lawrence (prob). [Private rec of Joe V Wright, Haverford PA (1979); 1790 & 1800 Censuses]

JOHN 23 m (License) 16 May 1760 **Mary Brady.**
[WRIGHT MARR, 55]

JOHN 24 m (License) 22 Dec 1761 **Jane Nixon.**
[WRIGHT MARR, 55]

JOHN 25 of Mt Pleasant NY m **Ruth Cheesman.** Issue: John, Samuel, Benjamin, Joseph M, Susanna, Deborah, Nancy Anna 1785 m Daniel Washburn, Tempy. Perh "John L" rec Mt Pleasant WestCoNY 1790 w/5 in fam. [Ada C. Haight's *Richard Washburn Family Genealogy*, 764; Query 9729 *Transcript* 18 Jan 1935; 1790 Census]

JOHN 26 m (License) 8 Feb/14 Nov 1763 **Rachel Lawrence.** [WRIGHT MARR, 55]

JOHN 27 [John 15] m 1) (License) 8 Feb 1763 **Sarah VanWyck** m 2) (License) 4 Jan 1783 **Margaret Floyd.** [WRIGHT MARR, 55; WRIGHT/OB by Perrine]

JOHN 28 [John 13] b 25 Feb 1775. [WRIGHT RECORDS by Stark]

JOHN 29 Nine Partners tax list 1775-1779. [CRUM ELBOW TAX LISTS]

JOHN 30 of Rumbout Pct NY. Issue: Jenny and Rachel bp (Rumbout Presby Ch) 1767. [Rumbout Presby Ch Rec]

JOHN 31 m NY (License) 12 Jan 1780 **Catherine Somendyck.** [WRIGHT MARR, 55]

JOHN 32 [Jotham 3] b Peekskill NY 30 Nov 1782 d 31 Jan 1861 m 1810 **Sarah Jane McFarland** of New Rochelle NY. Coppersmith of NYC. (Brother of David 6). [WRIGHTS OF LONG ISLAND by Francis Wright]

JOHN 33 Clinton NY tax list (not in 1787). Perh rec Clinton DutCoNY 1790. [CRUM ELBOW TAX LISTS; 1790 Census]

JOHN 34 b 29 Mar 1729 d after 19 July 1803 m **Phebe Seaman.** Pvt PS NY. [DAR Patriot Index]

JOHN 35 [Matthew 1] b prob Otsego Co NY d ae 60 m **Susan Bassett.** Rev War and 1812 service. To AlbCoNY after marriage. Perh rec Westford, Otsego Co 1820. Later of Duanesburg Schenectady Co NY. Issue: John Y, Justus, Samuel, Fanny, Ebenezer, Jane. [HUDSON-MOHAWK VALLEY by Reynolds]

JOHN GROSBECK 36 [Thomas 2] b Eastchester NY 8 Jan 1757 d Eastchester NY Sep 1794 m 1) 17 Nov 1778 **Phoebe Bartow** b 1759 dau Anthony & Charity (Stevenson) Bartow m 2) her sister **Charity Bartow** b 1765. Surgeon's mate (Army hospital) in Rev. Physician, buys land 1785 of James Hunt. Perh rec Eastchester WestCoNY 1790 w/7 in fam. Adm 16 Sep 1794 to wid Charity. Issue: Deryck 1785 dsp, Grosbeck 1786 dsp, Susanna 1789 dsp, Hannah 1791 m Cornelius Stevenson Bartow. [Kings Co NY PR 12:103; DutCoNY Deeds I:289; "The Bartow Pedigree" by E.P.B. in RECORD (1872), 3:31; WRIGHT/OB by Perrine]

JOHN 37 d Fishkill NY 20 Nov 1794 perh m Fishkill NY 14 Aug 1785 **Marritje Bush.** Farmer. Adm 4 June 1795 to Zachariah Bush of Fishkill. [DutCoNY PR Adm B:17; Fishkill RDC Rec]

JOHN 38 [David 4] b New Windsor NY 23/25 Feb 1786 d Florida, Orange Co NY 15 Apr 1838 m Newburgh NY 10 Apr 1810 **Phebe Halstead** dau Gershom & Mary (Smith) Halstead. To Florida NY by 1810. Soldier in War of 1812. Blacksmith. Issue: Francis Glow 1812, Henry Nelson 1813, Charlotte 1815, William Halstead 1818, Charles Jackson 1821, Benjamin Halstead 1823, Sarah Jane 1827, Anna Halstead 1831, Eliza Moore 1834. [WRIGHTS OF LONG ISLAND by Francis Wright, citing Bible Rec; "Halstead Corrections," in RECORD (1959) 90:244]

JOHN 39 [Ephraim 2] b 8 Jul 1788 d by 3 Mar 1797. [WRIGHT RECORDS by Stark]

JOHN 40 of Middleburg NY m **Annatye Eckerson**. Issue (bp Middleburg RDC): John Wright 1800. [IGI 84]

JOHN 41 [John 40] bp Middleburg (RDC) NY 26 Aug 1800. [IGI 84]

JOHN 42 [Robert 2] b 1801/2 liv 84 in 1886 m 2 Jun 1825 **Sally Ann Frost** b 25 Mar 1810 d 30 Dec 1880 dau Ezra & Mary (Wallace) Frost. Issue: Ebenezer d unm 1848, Edward 1826. [PUTNAM COUNTY HIST by Pelletreau, 240; FROST GEN, 166]

JOHN 43 m Dutchess Co NY (Hopewell Reformed Ch) 25 Dec 1824 **Delilah Kronk**. [Hopewell RDC Rec]

JOHN CALVIN 44 [Calvin 1], b 1802 d Schenectady NY 25 Jan 1862, m 1) Feb 1844 **Caroline Frost** d 27 Mar 1846 ae 41 dau James & Mary (March) Frost m 2) Esperance NY 17 June 1847 **Sarah W Bouck** who d Schenectady NY 19 Oct 1859. NY State Comptroller, sometime of Schoharie Co NY. Issue, 1 son: Nicholas Weed or Ford. [VRs in *Schoharie Patriot*; Query 1435 in *Transcript* 3 Aug 1910; WRIGHT MARR, 55]

JOHN PRATT 45 [Ephraim 13] b perh Kent NY 3 Mar 1797. [WRIGHT RECORDS by Stark]

JOHN S 46 [Samuel 10] b 9 Sept 1783 d Berne AlbCoNY 11 Jan 1858 ae 75 bur Berne (Wright Burying Ground) m **Miriam---** b ca 1783 d 9 June 1847. Rec Berne NY 1810-40; farmer of Berne 1850. Issue (from Census): Lotta, Hannah, Alvah, Silas, Margaret. [ALBANY COUNTY HIST by Parker, 101,180]

JOHN Y 47 [John 35]. b near Cooperstown NY, d Albany Co NY ae about 75 Rec AlbCoNY 1810,

Westerlo NY 1820. Issue: Justus, Henry, Charles, George, Sylvester, Ann, Eliza, Miranda. [HUDSON-MOHAWK FAMILIES by Reynolds, 1473]

JOHN 48 [Joseph 1] b 29 Mar 1729 d 25 Nov 1801. Issue: Obadiah. [WRIGHT/OB by Perrine]

JOHN 49 [Andrew 1] b perh Staten Island by 1747.

JOHN 50 [William 2] b 1778. Of Brooklyn NY.

JOHN 51 [Charles 5] b perh Somers WestCoNY.

JOHN 52 [David 6] b perh Newburgh NY 1821.

JOHN 53 [Isaac 4] b perh Hempstead LI 1834.

JOHN 54 [John 19] b perh New Windsor NY.

JOHN 55 [John 25]

JOHN 56 [Matthew 1] b perh Cooperstown NY.

JOHN 57 [Robert 2] b perh Carmel NY 1801.

JOHN 58 [William 24] b perh Poughkeepsie NY.

JOHN C 59 [Daniel 21] b 1848.

JOHN FORET 60 [John 17] b NYC 1813.

JOHN G 61 [Cruger 1] b 1822.

JOHN G 62 [Lewis 1] b 1824.

JOHN LOWNSBERRY 63 [William 14]

JOHN REED 64 [Abraham 7] b 1831.

JONAS 1 shipwright of NYC m **Catalina---**. Will 1 Nov 1770 proved 2 Feb 1773 named exec Wm McKinley of NY & Samuel Loudon of London.

Issue (from will): Samuel (bequest if he can be reached by mail), James (perh dec'd, his dau Sarah named), Peter, plus John (whose chn John Frett & Catherine are remembered). [NYCoNY PR 28:383 in NYHS 32:91]

JONATHAN 1 [George 1] of Flushing LI, b ca 1635 (aged 46 in 1681) prob d Flushing LI 1698 m perh 2) by 12 Dec 1694 **Sarah Saitley** dau Henry Saitley of Newtown NY. His will 5 Nov 1698 said proved same year. Her unrecorded will 19 Jan 1724/5 "proved" 7 Aug 1729 also names dau Mary Fish, gd Elizabeth Fish, Elizabeth Furman, gs Josiah Furman. Of Flushing by 1664. Deeded land in Rehoboth MA by father 2 Feb 1683/4, sold by him 27 Jun 1684 to John Doged. Issue (from his will): John, Charles, Job, Jonathan Jr 1674, David, Samuel, Richard, Henry, George, Maritiye Elizabeth m George Wood Jr, Sarah m Jacob Griffin, Hannah, Mary, Niantjie/Nancy 1698. [(Jonathan's will) NYCoNY PR 5-6:275 in NYHS 25:300, (Sarah's will) 35:138; *Early Rehoboth* by Richard LeBaron Bowen (1948), 3:146-150; Notes of Mary K Witherbee (1979)]

JONATHAN 2 [Jonathan 1] b 1674 d Flushing LI 26 Feb 1742 m **Wyntie/Winifred Simonds/Symonds**. His will as "Jonathan Sr" 11 Oct 1742 proved 9 Mar 1743. Her will 24 Oct 1744 proved 15 Feb 1744/5 exec David Roe, Ezekiel Roe, Benjamin Wright. Of Flushing 1705, sells land in Westchester to Wm Betts. Carpenter of Eastchester NY 1721, sells land in Eastchester, to Moses Fowler. Issue (from both wills): Elizabeth m ----Wheeler, Catherine m Jacob Griffin/Grissom, Wyntie 1699 (not in will), Sarah, Susannah 1709 (unm 1745), Jonathan 1695 (not in will), Benjamin. [QueCoNY PR #243, Queens College, Flushing NY; DutCoNY Deeds C:352, E:306; NYCoNY PR 14:18 (Jonathan), 15:333 (Winifred) in NYHS 27:320, 28:32]

JONATHAN 3 [Jonathan 2] bp Flushing LI 1695 perh the "Capt Jonathan" who d Newtown NY 26 Feb 1744. ["Family of Jonathan Wright of Flushing, L.I. as deduced from sources collected to date," by Mary K. Witherbee (March 1979); WRIGHT/FL by Perrine]

JONATHAN 4 of Woodbridge NJ d by 1758 m **Hannah Bloomfield** b Woodbridge NJ 29 Dec 1725. She m 2) Jonathan Brooks. Her bro Ezekiel Bloomfield d 1757/8 m Elizabeth Skinner dau **Wright Skinner** who, with his bro/law Jonathan Brooks adm Jonathan Wright's est. ["Thomas Bloomfield of Woodbridge NJ" by William Jones, in RECORD (1937), Vol 68]

JONATHAN 5 [John 2] d Flushing LI 1784 m 28 Oct 1737 **Amy Hazzard** d 23 Aug 1757 wid of Nathaniel Hazzard dau Richard & Hannah Allsopp. Will 4 Jun 1779 proved 11 Aug 1784 names daus, [nephews] Stephen & Richard Drake. Issue (from will): Melicent m Thomas Hunt, Hannah m 1) Moses Drake m 2) Thomas Hunt. [NYCoNY PR 37:120 in NYHS 36:373; WRIGHT/FL by Perrine; *Andrew Warde and His Descendants* by Geo K Warde (1910), 612]

JONATHAN 6 [Samuel 5] b 13 Mar 1745 d 15 Apr 1835 m 27 Jun 1784 **Tryphena Tracy** b Apr 1748 d 20 Nov 1786. [Private Bible record, Charlene F. Bryan, Sherburne NY]

JONATHAN 7 b Flushing LI 1745. Enlisted in Capt Daniel Wright's QueCoNY Militia 4 May 1761. Laborer. [NY Muster Rolls in NYHS Vol 24]

JONATHAN 8 of Fishkill m **Elizabeth---**. Notice: "Jonathan Jr will pay no debts she contracts." [*New York Mercury* 4 Oct 1762]

JONATHAN 9 tavernkeeper of Frederickburgh DutCoNY 9 Jul 1784, named adm of brother Jacob's (of Flushing) estate. [NYCoNY Adm, in

NYHS 36:412

JONATHAN 10 [Samuel 4] b 1774. No further record.

JONATHAN 11 of Philipse Pct 1777. [Philipse Pct Tax List 1777, in PUTNAM COUNTY HIST by Pelletreau, 127]

JONATHAN 12 of Dutchess Co NY then (before Rev) of Wheatley LI, b 17 Mar 1737, d 1820 m 1) 5 Mar 1760 **Patience Wheeler** (d 7 Feb 1770) m 2) 16 Feb 1772 **Ethelannah Frost**. Will 2 Jul 1820 proved 22 Nov 1820. Issue: Frances ("Fanny" in will) 1765 m Duncan Fowler, Derius 1768 (not in will), Patience 1773 m Aaron Van Nostrand, Frost 1775 m Gerry Springsteen, William 1782 m Zippora Baldwin, Isaac 1784. ["Family Bible of Jonathan Wright of Flushing, Hempstead LI", in NYS DAR Bible Rec 46:100,101; Private record, Jeanne Bender, Evansville IN]

JONATHAN 13 of Franklin, Dutchess Co NY bo't Lot 535, Berne (originally to Daniel Champenois, then 1799 to Andrew Brown and P. Todd), 25 Nov 1803. Perh rec Berne NY 1810. [Stephen Van Rensselaer Survey Book, NY State Archives, Albany NY]

JONATHAN 14 of Berne NY, m Rhinebeck (RDC) NY 11 Feb 1783 **Mary Annah Bartow/Bartoe** b 21 Jun 1764 bp (adult) Berne (Beaver Dam RDC) NY 17 Jun 1798. Leased Lot 520 in Berne 17 Jan 1795; rec Berne 1800, 1810. Issue: 3 sons, 3 daus before 1800. [Rhinebeck RDC Rec, Beaver Dam RDC Rec]

JONATHAN 15 m Flushing (St George Ch) NY 20 Oct 1799 **Catherine Rowe**. [St George's Ch Marriages in RECORD, 110:2]

JONATHAN 16 [Joseph 10]

JORDON F 1 [Isaac 4]

JOSEPH 1 [Adam 1] d 1739 m 1) (License) 1 Jan 1694 **Ann Henry** of Cedar Swamp LI m 2) (License) 1737/8 **Temperance Kirk** wid of Arthur Kirk dau Benjamin & Martha (Titus) Seaman liv 1738. Will 13 Nov 1738 proved 28 Feb 1738/9. Res Westbury LI. Issue (from will): Mary m Jeremiah Birch, Adam, Joseph, John 1729, Charles, Job. See JOSEPH 6. [NYCoNY PR 13:162 in NYHS 27:240; WRIGHT/OB by Perrine; WRIGHT MARR, 54]

JOSEPH 2 [Caleb 1] m **Freelove Weeks**. [WRIGHT/OB by Perrine]

JOSEPH 3 mariner of NYC prob dsp after 2 Oct 1740 (will) naming Ch of Eng in NYC sole legatee. [NYCoNY PR 14:18 in NYHS 27:320]

JOSEPH 4 [Adam 4] dsp Jericho, Oyster Bay LI 1768. Will 11 Jun 1768 proved 17 July 1768 names mother Elizabeth, sis Sarah, Almy, Deborah, bro Gilbert, Benjamin, William. [NYCoNY PR 26:359 in NYHS 31:193]

JOSEPH 5 of Flushing LI. Prob m Newtown (Presby Ch) LI 13 Jun 1728 **Bridget Hallett** dau Samuel Hallett of Newtown LI. Hallett's 1752 will names dau Bridgett Wright. Joseph's will 23 Oct 1784 proved 6 Dec 1785 names (besides ch Joseph, Samuel, Hallett dec'd) grchn James (son of Joseph), John Day, Hannah Day, Ann Day (all under age), Joseph Wood, Samuel Wood. Issue: Joseph (eldest), Samuel, Hallett dec'd. [Hallett Will NYCoNY PR 19:384 in NYHS 29:99]

JOSEPH 7 Nine Partners NY tax list Feb 1753-Jun 1756. [CRUM ELBOW TAX LISTS]

JOSEPH 8 DutCoNY witness (with Dirck Brinkerhoff) 13 May 1757 to will of Edward Churchill of Rumbout. [ALBANY WILLS, 287]

JOSEPH 9 m NYC (Presby Ch) 10 Aug 1771 **Mary Lashly**. Taylor. [1st/2nd Presby Ch Rec in RECORD; WRIGHT MARR, 55]

JOSEPH 10 b say 1770 d Milan, Dutchess Co NY, 10 Jul 1846, m (as "Joseph Right") Stanford (Bangall Bapt Ch) NY 10 Feb 1795 **Amy Mott** b 1771 d 1856 dau Joseph Mott. Of Freehold Greene Co 1800 and 1810, Milan Dutchess Co 1820. Will 29 Jun 1846 proved 28 Sep 1846. Issue (from will): Joseph M (of Union, Broome Co NY), Benjamin (of Union), Addison (of Union), Isaac (of Union), Jonathan (of Milan), George (of Milan), William (of Milan), Polly wf Judah Allen, Rebecca wf William Everett, Amy wf Samuel West, Anna A wf Frederick Fiester. [DutCoNY PR #3999; Private rec of Vincent Wright, Maitland FL (1979)]

JOSEPH 11 [Jacob 2] of Fishkill. Said killed in Rev 1778 in Light Horse Co. [WRIGHT/FL by Perrine]

JOSEPH 12 [William 1] d by 26 Dec 1809 m by 1781 **Sarah Mede**. Perh rec Philipstown NY 1790 w/5 in fam. See father's will. Issue (bp Fishkill RDC): Elizabeth 1781, William 1783, Jacob 1790. [Fishkill RDC Rec; 1790 Census]

JOSEPH 13 of Green Co NY [David 1752] b say 1785 m **Mary Halstead** b 1 Mar 1786 dau Gershom Halstead and sis of Phebe [qv]. Mary m 2) Ralph Sweet m 3) Thomas Smith. ["Halstead Corrections," in RECORD, 90:243; WRIGHT OF LONG ISLAND by Francis Wright, 14]

JOSEPH 14 [Joseph 5] living 23 Oct 1784, named "eldest" in father's will.

JOSEPH 15 of Beekman NY, farmer, d by 15 May 1797 (date of funeral) m **Catherine---**. Adm to wid 1 Sep 1797. [DutCoNY PR Adm B:75]

JOSEPH 16 [John 22] b prob Berne NY 2 Aug 1795

d 13 Aug 1881 bur So Berne (Rural Cem) NY m Berne 13 Oct 1814 **Phebe Wright** dau Samuel & Margaret (Wilsey) Wright. Farmer Berne NY 1850. Sold part of Lot 501 to Wm J Wright 1838. Issue: Chauncey, Edward, Jervis (twin), Jason (twin), Elvin, Lucretia, Alvah K. [AlbCoNY Deeds 106:195; Private record, Joe V Wright, Haverford PA (1979)]

JOSEPH 17 [Abijah 1] living 1812, named in will of gf Benjamin Wright. Perh "Joseph (at Mr Mondly's)" who had an acct with Dr Cornelius 27 Apr 1792 to 31 Dec 1803. [WRIGHT/FL by Perrine; CORNELIUS LEDGER]

JOSEPH 18 [Elijah 3] of Po'keepsie NY, dsp, m Pleasant Valley NY, 2 Oct 1833 **Eliza B. Southwick** b ca 1811, d NYC 2 Feb 1866 ae 54 dau Zadock Southwick. Her will proved 20 Oct 1870 names many Southwicks. [VRs in Po'keepsie Journal; DutCoNY PR #6200 1/2 also #5697, W:434-40]

JOSEPH 19 m Rhinebeck (RDC) NY 9 Sept 1807 **Hannah Hart.** [Rhinebeck RDC Rec]

JOSEPH 20 d Durham, Greene Co NY, 7 May 1835, m **Emeline---**. Will mentions only wife and father (not named) of Newburgh NY. [GreCoNY PR #480-10618, C:446]

JOSEPH FOWLER 21 [Simon 1] b Cortlandt NY 11 Nov 1800 d NYC 17 May 1832 m 30 Jul 1828 **Emeline Palelia Leak.** [SCJ, 352]

JOSEPH H 22 [Jacob 7 ?] of Fishkill, b Fishkill NY 4 Jan 1762 perh bp Rumbout (St George's Ch, Hempstead) NY 14 Jun 1762 living 1833. Enlisted 1777 (while living at home of Theodore Adriance) in Rev. After Rev lived Po'keepsie, Beekman, Fishkill. [Rejected Military Pension R-11897; St George's Ch Rec in RECORD, 11:49]

JOSEPH J 23 perh of Albany NY, b ca 1796 d 1 Aug 1858 ae 62. [Munsell's *Annals of Albany*, Vol 10]

JOSEPH 24 [Jacob 2] d in Revolution.

JOSEPH C 25 [David 10] b 1835.

JOSEPH CHEESMAN 26 [Samuel 13] b 1790.

JOSEPH M 27 [Joseph 10]. Of Union, Broome Co NY.

JOSEPHINE 1 [Abraham 7]

JOSHUA 1 Dutchess Co NY yeoman, d by 14 May 1785, m **Mary---**, adm to wid. [NYCoNY Adm in NYHS Vol 38]

JOSHUA 2 of Berne NY, b ca 1798 m **Margaret---**, living Berne 1850. Issue (from Census): Jacob, Richard, Mary, Amasa. [1850 Census]

JOSHUA 3 witn Nov 1781 to will of Barent Slaight, RichCoNY.

JOSHUA R 4 [Richard 2]

JOSIAH 1 [Enos 1] b ca Jul 1821 d 20 Sep 1840 ae 19-2-18 bur Fishkill RDC. [FISHKILL TOMBSTONES]

JOTHAM 1 of Rye NY shipjoiner, buys land in Rye, of Thomas Wright 1771. [DutCoNY Deeds H:351]

JOTHAM 2 [Edmund 2] b Oyster Bay 1708 d 20 Jul 1777 m **Tabiatha Sammis** of Huntington LI. Named in father's 1731 will. Issue: Jotham, Sarah m Joseph Latham, Samuel 1761, Augustus 1765. [WRIGHT/OB by Perrine]

JOTHAM 3 [Jotham 2] b Rye NY said d Terrytown NY m Peekskill NY 30 Nov 1778 **Elizabeth**

Dusenbury. 1st Lieut in Continental army. See Jotham 1. Issue: David 1779, Eliza 1780, John 1782, Sally bp 1787 (NY Presby Ch). [WRIGHT/OB by Perrine; NY Presby Ch Rec in RECORD, 20:38]

JUDITH1 [Anthony 2]

JULIA 1 [Daniel 21] b 1848.

JULIA ANN 2 [Jacob 11]

JULIA ANN 3 [Jacob 14]

JUSTUS 1 [Daniel 13] b prob Clinton NY ca 1790/1 d Freeman, Steuben Co NY 1866/71 m **Anna Cunningham** dau Frederick Cunningham. [Private Record, Mary K Witherbee, Oneonta NY (1979)]

JUSTUS 2 [John 35] m Coeymans NY 1811 **Betsey Langford**. Prob rec AlbCoNY 1820. From Coeymans NY to New Garden OH 1838. Issue: David 1817, Thomas, Ann. ["Duanesburg Quaker Records", in *Utah Genealogical and Historical Magazine* 4:48; "Coeymans Monthly Meeting Rec" in Hannay Papers]

JUSTUS 1 [John 47]

K L

Katherine (Nelson) wf [George 7]

KEZIAH 1 [Job 1] d 12 Apr 1731 m **John Burr**. [FROST GEN, 27; WRIGHT/OB by Perrine]

KEZIAH 2 [Jacob 1] m **Samuel Frost** b 25 Feb 1706 son William & Hannah (Pryer) Frost. Res Oyster Bay LI. Issue: Samuel, Keziah, Philena, Deborah, Sarah, Rhoda, Jacob, Ruth. [FROST GEN, 27; WRIGHT/OB by Perrine]

Keziah (Sammis) wf [Daniel 3]

LAURA 1 [Jacob 11]

LAURENCE 1 [Samuel 10] b 19 Aug 1790 prob m Berne NY ca 1832 **Roxanna----** b 16 Feb 1812, and both bp St Paul's Evang Luth Ch Berne NY 15 Apr 1832. [St Paul's Evang Luth Ch Rec, 14]

LAWRENCE 2 [John 22] of Berne NY. No records. [So according to Joe V Wright, Haverford PA (1979)]

LAWRENCE 3 [Cruger 1] b 1818.

LAURETTA M 1 [Cruger 1] b 1820.

LEONARD SLOTE 1 [Daniel 19]

LETITIA 1 [Gideon 4]

LETITIA 2 [Jacob 2]

LETSON 1 [William 14]

LEVERICH 1 [? Job 1] m (int rec) Jamaica (Grace Ch) LI 10 Aug 1730 **Martha Phillips.** [Grace Ch Rec]

LEWIS 1 [Thomas 8] b LaGrange NY 1800 d LaGrange NY 14 Apr 1887 m 1) 3 Nov 1820 **Maria Vermiya** b 16 Sep 1801 d 30 Dec 1827 dau John G & Elizabeth (Asten) Vermiya m 2) 13 Nov 1828 **Zilla Anderson** b 24 Feb 1799 d Nov 1855 dau John Anderson. Issue: Mary 1821, John G 1824, Abraham 1826, Ann Elizabeth 1830, Thomas 1833, Susan Ann 1834, Anderson 1838. [WRIGHT/FL by Perrine]

LEWIS BARTON 2 [Simon 1] b 1809.

Lois (Green) wf [Abraham 5]
Lovina (Sutherland) wf [Daniel 5]

LOTTA 1 [John 46] b 1805.

LOUISA 1 [Daniel 21] b 1840.

LOUISA 2 [Gilbert 4] b 1841.

LOUISE 1 [Matthew 1]

LUCINDA 1 [Wise 2] b 1842.

LUCRETIA 1 [James 20]

LUCRETIA 2 [Joseph 16]

LUCY ANN 1 [Isaac 3]

Lucy (White) wf [James 21]

LYDIA 1 [Samuel 10] b 18 June 1785 m Bethlehem (RDC) NY 5 Oct 1802 **Gabriel Barton** b ca 1775 d ca 1839 son Caleb Barton. Issue: Caleb, William. [BARTON GEN]

LYDIA 2 [Jacob 7] b say 1756 bp Rumbout (St George's Ch, Hempstead) NY 14 Jun 1762 with other f and other chn. [St George's Ch Rec, in RECORD, 11:49]

LYDIA 3 of Fishkill, m Dutchess Co NY, ca 22 May 1816 **Isaac Smith** of Frederickstown. [POUGHKEEPSIE M&D by Reynolds]

LYDIA 4 [George 4] b 1797.

LYDIA 5 [William 14]

Lydia (Cobbit) wf [Thomas 1]

LYMAN 1 [Richard 2] b 1824.

M

MARCUS 1 [William 13]

Magdelen (Kipp) wf [Jesse 1]

MARGARET 1 [Zebulon 1] b 1741 d 3 May 1828 m 1) **Noah Townsend** m 2) (License) 20 Mar 1765 **Daniel Thorne** b Oyster Bay 1726 d Oyster Bay 26 May 1781 m 3) **John Jackson.** Thorne's will made & proved 26 Mar 1781. No issue by Thorne. ["Early History of the Thorne Family," by Thorne Dickinson, in RECORD (1964), 95:149]

MARGARET 2 [Elijah 2] b by 31 Dec 1803 named in father's acct with Dr Cornelius. [CORNELIUS LEDGER]

MARGARET 3 [Daniel 13] prob b Albany Co NY by 1800 m ---**Hubbard** widower of her sister Anna [qv]. [Private record, Mary K Witherbee, Oneonta NY (1979)]

MARGARET 4 [William 4] bp Flushing (St George's Ch) LI 2 Nov 1806. [St George's Ch Rec]

MARGARET 5 [Isaac 3]

MARGARET 6 [Jacob 11]

MARGARET 7 [John 46] b 1822.

MARGARET 8 [Richard 2]

MARGARET 9 [William 24]

MARGARET J 10 [Daniel 21] b 1848.

Margaret (---) wf [Joshua 2]
Margaret (---) wf [Thomas 17]
Margaret (Bennet) wf [Jesse 2]
Margaret (Floyd) wf [John 27]
Margaret (Henry) wf [William 7]
Margaret (Marsh) wf [William 11]
Margaret (Urquehart) Shay wf [Gideon 2]
Margaret (Wilsey) wf [Samuel 10]
Margaret (Williams) wf [Uriah 2]
Margaret (Woodhull) wf [David 5]
Margery (Sloat) wf [William 13]
Maria (Vermilya) wf [Lewis 1]
Marian (Cunningham) wf [Robert 2]
Mariel (Hathaway) wf [James 17]

MARITIYE ELIZABETH 1 [Jonathan 1] m prob **George Wood**. George & Elizabeth sell land 17 Dec 1692 deeded them by [her] gf Henry Sawtles. 20 Dec 1692 one Henry Sawtell deeds house, land in Newtown to gs George Wood. Rec Flushing 1698 Census. Will of mother Sarah Wright names dau Elizabeth Wood. [NEWTOWN MINUTES, 2:383, 461-2]

MARK 1 m (License) 7 Oct 1783 **Sarah Magra**. [WRIGHT MARR, 56]

MARRON 1 [Benjamin 4] b prob Somers NY 16 Feb 1813 d 28 Oct 1865. [WRIGHT/FL by Perrine]

MARTHA See also MARTHYE, MARITIYE.

MARTHA 1 [Nicholas 2] m **Nathaniel Coles**. Issue: Nathaniel m Rose Wright. [COLE GEN]

MARTHA 2 [Abraham 1] b WestCoNY 21 Mar 1744 d 9 Mar 1834 m **Joseph Osborne** b Ridgefield *CT* [says Frost Gen] 11 Jun 1737 d Somers NY 26 Sep 1796. Of Ridgefield *NJ* acc to Perrine. Issue: Samuel liv 1791 (named in gf Wright's will), David 1769, Ozias 1771, Benjamin, Elizabeth, Ebenezer. [WRIGHT/FL by Perrine; FROST GEN, 74]

MARTHA 3 [Ephraim 1] b Windham CT 14 Jun 1733 m Hebron CT 11 Aug 1751 **Thomas Skinner** b 5 May 1731. Issue: Abel 1752, Martha 1753, Hannah 1755, Ephraim 1756, Ann 1758, Durthany 1767. ["Lt John Skinner" by Zoeth Skinner Eldridge, in REGISTER (1899) 53:402]

MARTHA 4 m (License) 28 Jan 1762 **Thomas Dickson.** [WRIGHT MARR, 56]

MARTHA 5 m (License) 4 Jan 1765 **Joseph Latting.** [WRIGHT MARR, 56]

MARTHA 6 of Poughkeepsie NY, m 16 Feb 1769 **William Walker.** [Poughkeepsie RDC Rec]

MARTHA 7 [Benjamin 1] b 22 Jun 1771 d 21 Oct 1860 m WestCoNY 21 May 1789 **Joel Frost** b 28 Sep 1765 d 28 Sep 1827 son John & Huldah (Munson) Frost. [SCJ, 374; FROST GEN, 75; WRIGHT MARR, 56]

MARTHA 8 [Daniel 16]

MARTHA 9 [Isaac 8]

MARTHA 10 [Wise 2]

Martha **(Davenport)** wf [Samuel 7]
Martha **(Denton** wf [James 1]
Martha **(Dodge)** wf [Stephen 2]
Martha **(Fordham)** wf [Benjamin 5]
Martha **(Knowels)** wf [Samuel 5]
Martha **(Phillips)** wf [Leverich 1]

MARVIN 1 [Isaac 4] b 1816.

MARY 1 said m **Thomas Horton** b Rye NY ca 1691 son David & Esther (King) Horton. To White Plains NY. Issue: Thomas 1758, Mary, David. [HORTON GEN, 4]

MARY 2 [Jonathan 1] perh m 1) **Josiah Furman** perh m 2) ---**Fish.** Mary Wright rec with father in 1698 Flushing census. Josiah Furman Sr & Mary deed 3 Jan 1692 and 1691-5 to sons Josiah Jr, Jonathan, Samuel. Will of Sarah Wright (wid Jonathan) 1724 names dau Mary Fish & gch Elizabeth Fish, Elizabeth Furman, Josiah Furman. [NYCoNY PR in NYHS 35:138; NEWTOWN MINUTES, 228, 246, 379, 436, 465, 517, 565]

Widow MARY 3 m Jamaica LI 12 Jul 1722 **Thomas Howell**. [WRIGHT MARR, 57]

MARY 4 of Hempstead LI m (licensed and certified) Jamaica (Grace Ch) LI 26 Mar 1728 **Jonas Sparks**. [Grace Ch Rec]

MARY 5 [Joseph 1] unm Nov 1738, perh m **Jeremiah Birch** of Oyster Bay [per Perrine], perh m **Samuel Willis** b 12 Feb 1721 son William & Hannah (Powell) Willis [per Haight]. [WRIGHT/OB by Perrine; *Richard Washburn Family Genealogy* by Ada C. Haight, 1228]

MARY 6 [Reuben 2]. No further record. [WRIGHT/FL by Perrine]

MARY 7 m **Stephen Horton** b White Plains NY ca 1749 son Daniel & Esther (Lane) Horton. [HORTON GEN, 5]

MARY 8 m (License) 8 Dec 1759 **George Harvey**. [WRIGHT MARR, 57]

MARY 9 [James 4] b perh New Castle NY 7 Jan 1761 m **Jesse Simons**. [WRIGHT/OB by Perrine]

MARY 10 m (License) 16 Nov 1764 **John Brien**. [WRIGHT MARR, 57]

MARY 11 m (License) 11 Oct 1782 **Loris Noe**. [WRIGHT MARR, 57]

MARY 12 m WestCoNY 14 Aug 1786 **Henry Palmer**. [SCJ, 373; WRIGHT MARR, 57]

MARY 13 [Robert 1 ?] m Westchester Co NY 15
Mar 1792 **Jeremiah Maybie**. He had an acct with
Dr Cornelius 1 Apr 1799 to Jan 1804. [SCJ,
376; CORNELIUS LEDGER]

MARY 14 [William 1] living and m by 26 Dec
1809, ---**Beaumont** supposedly an English
officer. Perh settled near Lake Champlain.
Mary Beaumont named in father's will. [DutCoNY
PR D:125; WRIGHT/FL by Perrine]

MARY 15 of Berne NY, m **John Hayes** b ca 1761 d
24 Apr 1849. Issue (bp Beaver Dam RDC): Mary
1794, Thomas 1796, Nancy 1797, Maria 1799.
[Henry Cody Genealogical Records, Old Stone
Fort Cem, Schoharie NY]

MARY 16 [John 13] b 9 May 1777 (twin of
Rachel). [WRIGHT RECORDS by Stark]

MARY 17 [Elijah] of Pleasant Valley NY, m Dec
1821 **Joseph A Lattin** son Nathaniel & Sally
Lattin. Of Barre, Orleans Co NY 1837. Issue
(from Elijah Wright's will): Elijah Belden
Lattin liv 1837. [POUGHKEEPSIE M&D by
Reynolds; DutCoNY PR #3519]

MARY 18 [Joseph 2] b by 1738.

MARY 19 [Anthony 2] of Staten Island

MARY 20 [Anthony 4] of Worcester Co MD

MARY 21 [Benjamin 3] of Huntington LI

MARY 22 [Dennis 2] of Oyster Bay

MARY 23 [Elijah 1]

MARY 24 [William 2] b 1780.

MARY 25 [William 8] b 1790.

MARY 26 [Samuel 13] b NYC 1792.

MARY 27 [Enos 1] b 1802/3.

MARY 28 [Lewis 1] b 1821.

MARY 29 [George 7] b 1841.

MARY 30 [Gideon 2] of Oyster Bay

MARY 31 [Isaac 2] of Hempstead

MARY 32 [John 1] of Oyster Bay

MARY 33 [John 19] of New Windsor

MARY 34 [Joshua 2] of Berne

MARY 35 [Stephen 4] b 1842.

MARY ANN 36 [Gilbert 5] b 1834.

MARY ANN 37 [Robert 2] of Carmel

MARY ANN 38 dau [Caleb 4] of Carmel

MARY C 39 [Isaac 7] b ca 1832.

MARY EMELINE 40 [Solomon 3] of WestCo

MARY L 41 [Abraham 7] of Pleasant Valley

Mary (---) wf [Henry 1]
Mary (---) wf [George 2]
Mary (---) wf [David 4]
Mary (---) wf [Elijah 3]
Mary (---) wf [Joshua 1]
Mary (---) wf [Jacob 7]
Mary (Barton) wf [John 22]
Mary Annah (Bartow) wf [Jonathan 14]
Mary Ann (Cunningham) wf [Caleb 4]
Mary (Davenport) wf [George 7]
Mary (Dennis) wf [Adam 1]
Mary Ann (Forman) wf [Benjamin 12]
Mary (Fowler) wf [Simon 1]
Mary (Halstead) wf [Joseph 13]

Mary (Hamilton) wf [Isaac 2]
Mary (Hawkhurst) wf [Solomon 2]
Mary (Jaycocks) wf [Daniel 20]
Mary (Jones) wf [William 29]
Mary (Lashly) wf [Joseph 9]
Mary (Leverich) wf [Job 3]
Mary (McQuirrey) wf [Thomas 7]
Mary (Nelson) wf [Daniel 13]
Mary (Seaman) wf [Nathaniel 8]
Mary (Skidmore) wf [Nathaniel 3]
Mary (Slote) wf [Daniel 19]
Mary (Townsend) wf [John 1]
Mary (Vail) wf [Nathan 2]
Mary (Underhill) wf [Horatio 1]
Mary (Warren) wf [Abram 1]
Mary (Wood) wf [David 10]
Maryitje (Bush) wf [John 37]

MARYTHE 1 [Job 6] living 4 May 1783, named in father's will. [NYCoNY PR in NYHS 36:211]

MATILDA 1 [William 2] b 1787.

MATTHEW 1 b Chatham? CT ca 1700/7 d Cooperstown, Otsego Co NY 1810 ae 103 m **Esther Lewis**, d Cooperstown NY 1820 ae 90. Issue: Daniel, John, Earl, Matthew, Thomas, Ebenezer, Sally, Esther, Hepseber, Louise, 2 others. [HUDSON-MOHAWK VALLEYS by Reynolds, 1473-4]

MATTHEW 2 [Matthew 1]

MELICENT See also MILLICENT.

MELICENT/MILSESON 1 [Jonathan 5] d 15 Sep 1802 m 20 Jan 1758 **Thomas Hunt** of Hunt's Point LI. [WRIGHT/FL by Perrine]

MELICENT 2 [Benjamin 4] b prob Somers NY 22 Feb 1796 d 19 Apr 1830 m **Rev John Bailey** of Highland Falls NY. [WRIGHT/FL by Perrine]

Meliscent (Halsey) wf [Allison 1]

MERCY 1 [Nicholas 2] m **Robert Coles**. [WRIGHT/OB by Latting]

Mercy Ann (Horton) wf [Isaac 4]

MERIAM 1 [Daniel 13] b Albany Co NY ca 1796 prob d Oxford, Chenango Co NY 10 Jan 1858 ae 63 m **John Carhart Jr.** [Private record, Mary K Witherbee, Oneonta NY (1979)]

MICAJAH/MICAIJAH 1 [Daniel 3] b 11 Dec 1764 d Somers NY 3 Mar 1811 m 6 Sep 1787 **Ruth Miller** d 30 May 1811 ae 50 bur Somers NY dau Increase & Abigail (Crampton) Miller of Lebanon NJ. Leather dresser and glove maker. Rec Stephentown WestCoNY 1790 w/5 in fam. Account with Dr Cornelius Mar 1781 to Dec 1805 names "bro James." Mortg farm in Stephentown (bounded by Daniel Wright decd) 29 Jun 1792. Will 9 Oct 1798 bequeaths all to wf Ruth for benefit of chn. Issue: Rachel 1789 m Isaac Candee, Daniel 1790, Charles 1792, Elizabeth 1794 m James Phillips, James 1799. [WRIGHT/FL by Perrine; 1790 Census; CORNELIUS LEDGER; WestCoNY Mortg E:111; FROST GEN, 339]

MILLICENT 1 [Daniel 3] b 19 Feb 1770 d 14 Oct 1847 m (at her bro Micaijah Wright's house) WestCoNY 30 Apr 1788 **David Beadle** b 25 Mar 1764 d 23 Jun 1848 son Ephraim & Philena (Frost) Beadle/Bedell of Yorktown NY. His will proved 23 Jun 1848 bequeathes $1000 to Milicent Knapp dau Joseph who m his wf's sister Hannah Wright. [SCJ, 372; FROST GEN, 75]

Millicent (Purdy) wf [Benjamin 1]

MILTON H 1 [George 7] b 1834.

MINNIE 1 [Isaac 7]

MINNIE 2 [William 24]

MIRANDA 1 [John 47]

MIRAM 1 of Albany Co NY m by 1800 **William McIntosh**. Issue (bp Bethlehem (RDC) NY): Elizabeth 1801, Stephen 1802. [BETHLEHEM REC, 11,19]

Miriam (---) wf [John 46]
Miriam (Woolsey) wf [Enos 1]

MORDECAY 1 [Peter 1] b 1649 d 1650. [WRIGHT/OB by Perrine]

N

NANCY 1 "Write" m Fishkill NY 31 Dec 1788 **Isaac Meed**. [Fishkill RDC Rec]

NANCY ANNA 2 [John 25] b 17 Jan 1785 d 8 Mar 1824 m **Daniel Washburn** b Mt Pleasant, WestCoNY 17 Nov 1779 d 14 Jul 1813 son Daniel & Phylena (Matthews) Washburn. Issue: Abraham 1806, Isaac 1808, Philena Wright 1810, Jacob Cheesman 1812. [Ada C. Haight's *Richard Washburn Family Genealogy*, 765; Query 9729 by V.B.S., in *Transcript* 18 Jan 1935]

NANCY 3 [William 8] b 1790.

NANCY E 4 [Jacob 11]

Nancy (---) wf [Gilbert 3]
Nancy (---) wf [Gilbert 4]
Nancy B **(Green)** wf [Ebenezer 5]

NAOMI 1 [Samuel 4] b ca 1772 m **Moses Hull** b ca 1768. [Private record, Janette MacEntire, Preston ID (1979)]

Naomy **(Barker)** wf [Richard 1]
Naomi **(Young)** wf [Thomas 10]

NATHAN 1 [Reuben 2] b by 23 Jan 1803, named in Dr Cornelius' Ledger. [CORNELIUS LEDGER]

NATHAN/NATHANIEL 2 [Jacob 2] d Somers NY ca 1808 m **Mary Vail** b 15 Oct 1766. Perh "Nathaniel" rec Stephentown WestCoNY 1790 w/9 in fam. Issue (among others ?): Nathaniel. [Ada C. Haight's *Richard Washburn Family Genealogy*, 178-179; WRIGHT/FL by Perrine; 1790

Census]

NATHANIEL 3 [David 2] b say 1755 d South Hempstead NY 1785 m **Mary Skidmore**. Will 5 May 1785 proved 10 Sept 1785 names bro David, bros/law Walter & Joseph Skidmore. Issue (from will): 2 sons not named, both under age in 1785. [NYCoNY PR 38:154 in NYHS 37:196; WRIGHTS OF LONG ISLAND, by Francis Wright]

NATHANIEL 4 [Samuel 4] b 1778 m **Sarah Shed** dau Daniel Shed. [Private record, Jannett MacEntire, Preston ID (1979); *Ancestry and Descendants of Jonathan Calkins Wright* by Istel L Wright (1958)]

NATHANIEL 5 [David 5] of New Windsor NY ?. [DAR Lineage Book 119:59]

NATHANIEL 6 [David 4]. Sold land at New Windsor NY and by 1823 lived at Windsor NY. [WRIGHTS OF LONG ISLAND by Francis Wright]

NATHANIEL 7 [Abijah 1] b by 13 Dec 1803, named in father's acct with Dr Cornelius. [CORNELIUS LEDGER]

NATHANIEL 8 [Nathaniel 2] m **Mary Seaman**. Res: Somers NY. Issue: Horace 1823, Eliza m Andrew Pell Sutton. [Ada C. Haight's *Richard Washburn Family Genealogy*, 178]

NATHANIEL 9 b WestCoNY ca 1765 d Bedeque PEI 25 Apr 1825 m Tryon PEI 25 Jan 1788 **Ann Lord** b Tryon PEI ca 1770 d Bedeque PEI 21 Mar 1839. See source for detail and extended line. See STEPHEN 5. [LOYALIST LINEAGES, 770]

NELSON 1 [George 7] b 1841.

NICHOLAS 1 of Co Norfolk Eng. Issue: Anthony, Nicholas, Peter. [WRIGHT/OB, by Latting]

NICHOLAS 2 [Nicholas 1] b prob Co Norfolk Eng

ca 1609/10 d Oyster Bay LI by Dec 1682 m by 1630 **Ann Beaupre** d Oyster Bay LI 1683. Emigrated Aug 1635 with bros Anthony & Peter to Lynn MA. Then Sandwich MA. To Oyster Bay LI 1653. Will 10 Apr 1674 (age 65) proved 13 Dec 1682, names wf Ann exec. Issue: Caleb, John 1636, Edmund, Rebecca m 1) Eleazer Leverich from whom div 1760 m 2) William Frost, Sarah m Josiah Latting, Deborah, Mercy m Robert Coles, Martha m Nathaniel Coles. [NYCoNY PR 1-2:449 in NYHS 25:121; WRIGHT/OB by Latting; *Winthrop-Babcock Genealogy* by J.L. Frost, 572]

NICHOLAS 3 [Edmund 2] of Oyster Bay, named in father's 1731 will.

NICHOLAS WEED 4 [John 44]

O

OBADIAH 1 [John 48] m (License) 24 May 1777 **Jane Sayre**. [WRIGHT/OB by Perrine; *The Sayre Family*, by Theodore M Banta (1901), 83; WRIGHT MARR, 57]

OBADIAH 2 [Dennis 2] bp 24 Feb 1739 d 27 Nov 1815 m **Sarah Adams** dau Nathan Adams. Res Westport CT. [WRIGHT/OB by Perrine]

OLIVE 1 [Daniel 21] b 1844.

OLNEY F 1 [Abel 1]

OPHELIA 1 [Abel 1]

ORRIN 1 [Wise 2] b 1833.

OSCAR 1 [William 25]

P

Patience (Bill) wf [Daniel 6]
Patience (Wheeler) wf [Jonathan 12]

PATTERSON 1 [Ambrose 1] b 1801.

PENELOPE 1 [Caleb 1] m **Daniel Reynolds.** [WRIGHT/OB by Perrine]

PERRY GARDINER 1 [David 10] b 1830.

PETER 1 [Nicholas 1] b Eng say 1590 drowned Virginia 1675 m perh Eng by 1635 [per Perrine] **Alice---** d Oyster Bay LI 24 Feb 1685 ae 70+. She m 2) Richard Crabb. Issue: Gideon 163-, Job 1636, Lydia m Isaac Horner, Hannah (d unm 1675, Sarah m Edmund Wright, Elizabeth, James, William 1641 (d 1648), Mary 1642 m Samuel Andrews, Mordecay 1649 (d 1650), Adam 1650, Peter (d 1651). Est adm by son Gideon 12 Apr 1675. [NYCoNY PR 1-2:109 in NYHS 25:28; WRIGHT/OB by Latting; "Wright Family," private MSS by Clara Wright Rathbun, Oneonta NY; Plymouth Records, 8:6]

PETER 2 b Hempstead LI 9 Jul 1740 d Bennington VT 7 Jun 1821 m Hempstead LI 9 Jul 1761 **Elizabeth Baker** b 28 Mar 1743 North Kingstown RI d 16 Aug 1819 ae 76-4-22. Lived Newport RI, then Shaftsbury VT ca 1779. Rev War service RI. Issue: Susannah 1762, John 1763, Hannah 1764, Samuel 1766, Daniel 1770, Mary, Deborah, Elizabeth, Joseph 1779, Peter 1780, Seaman 1782. [*The Wright Family. A Genealogical Record from 1740-1914 of the Descendants of Peter Wright (1740-1821)* by Fred Philo Wright (Oswego NY 1914)]

PETER 3 m (License) 18 Oct 1760 **Margaret Blooms**. [WRIGHT MARR, 58]

PETER 4 [John 16] No further record. [WRIGHT/FL by Perrine; DUTCHESS COUNTY HIST, 498]

PETER BICE 5 [Samuel 4] b 21 Jan 1776 d Dearborn Co IN 1825 m **Elizabeth Shed** dau Daniel & Lucy (Nutting) Shed. [Query 6391 in *Transcript*, 1 May 1933; Private record, Jannett MacEntire, Preston ID (1979); *Ancestry and Descendants of Jonathan Calkins Wright 1760-1958*]

PETER 6 [? Adam 3] said b Oyster Bay LI early 1700s d Botetourt Co VA 1793 m ca 1750 **Jane Hughart** prob d ca 1823 Bourbon Co KY dau James & Agnes (Jordon) Hughart. Moved from LI (with bro Thomas, but see THOMAS 18) to VA in Spring 1746. Settled Jackson's River VA. His will 12 Nov 1793 proved Dec 1793 Botetourt Co VA. 13 chn. [*Ancestors-Descendants of James Wilson Wright Sr, who married Cynthia Rebecca Jones, Paris, Bourbon County, Kentucky* by W.R. & R.L. McCann (1954), 5]

PETER 7 [Adam 1]

PETER 8 [Jonas 1]

PHABA 1 m (License) 21 Jul 1757 **Simon White**. [WRIGHT MARR, 58]

PHEBE See also PHABA.

PHEBE of Dutchess Co NY b say 1748 d ca 1790 m ca 1765 **Hendrick Wiltsie** b Dutchess Co NY 27 Mar 1746 son Henry Teunissen & Hester (Van Vleck) Wiltsie. Phebe Wright charged "Hendrick Woolsey" 1768 as father of her unborn child. He was prob of Clinton NY 1790, Berne NY 1800. Issue: Henricus 1768, Cornelius 1769, Reuben 1770 m Lucretia Hutchins,

Wyntje/Lavinia 1772, Henry Jr 1776 m Margaret Dempsey, John 1778, Eleanor 1780, Abraham 1782, Phoebe 1784, Jacob 1786 bp Berne (Beaver Dam Ch) NY 17 Jun 1788, William 1787 bp Berne (Beaver Dam Ch) NY 17 Jun 1788. [DutCoNY Ancient Records #7466; WILTSIE FAM in REGISTER, 107:213,214; Beaver Dam RDC Rec]

PHEBE 2 [Daniel 3] b 1775 d 19 Sep 1860 m 19 Jan 1792 **Gilbert Haviland** b 1757 d 21 Dec 1719. Issue: Esther 1794, Gilbert 1805, Daniel Wright 1806, Sarah Ann 1810, Ebenezer. [SCJ, 372; FROST GEN, 339]

PHEBE 3 [Job 6] living 4 May 1783, named in father's will.

PHEBE 4 [Samuel 10] b 27 Jul 1788, m prob Berne NY 1814 **Joseph Wright** b 1795 [qv]. [WRIGHT FAMILY RECORD contributed by Joe V Wright]

PHEBE 5 m Rhinebeck NY 16 Mar 1820 **David Burnet.** [IGI 84]

PHEBE 6 [David 1]

PHEBE 7 [George 4] b 1784.

PHEBE 8 [Robert 2] b 1798.

PHEBE 9 [Simon 1] b 1817.

PHEBE 10 [Isaac 3] of Fishkill

PHEBE 11 [James 4]

PHEBE 12 [Reuben 2] of Stephentown

PHEBE ANN 13 [Wise 2] b 1838

PHEBE ANN 14 [Isaac 8]

Phebe (---) wf [Isaac 8]

Phebe (Bartow) wf [John 36]
Phebe (Brown) wf [David 9]
Phebe (Burt) wf [Abraham 3]
Phebe (Cheesman) wf [Samuel 13]
Phebe (Gardiner) wf [David 10]
Phebe (Halstead) wf [John 38]
Phebe (Jackson) wf [Gilbert 2]
Phebe (Quimby) wf [Reuben 2]
Phebe (Seaman) wf [John 34]
Phebe (Yeomans) wf [Job 6]
Phebe (Warren) wf [Isaac 5]

PHILA 1 [Ambrose 1] b 1795.

PHILANDER [Wise 2] b 1831.

PHILENA 1 [John 9] m ---Warner/Waring. [WRIGHT/FL by Perrine]

PHILENA 2 [Benjamin 4] b prob Somers NY 1 Feb 1801 d 12 Jun 1860 m **Theodosius White** of Yorktown NY. [WRIGHT/FL by Perrine]

PHILO BRADLEY 1 [David 10] b 1834.

PLATT S 1 [William 13] b 1821.

POLLY 1 [Samuel 10] aka Mary b 26 Feb 1797 living 1831 unm. [Private Record, Joe V Wright, Haverford PA (1979)]

POLLY 2 [Thomas 11] bp Coxsackie (RDC) NY 1804. [IGI 84]

POLLY 3 [Joseph 10]

PRUDENCE 1 [John 9] Nothing further. [WRIGHT/FL by Perrine]

PURNELL 1 [Anthony 4]

R

RACHEL 1 [Job 1] b Oyster Bay 29 Jun 1689 m **Thomas Stokes.** [FROST GEN, 27; WRIGHT/OB by Perrine]

RACHEL 2 [Adam 3] m (License) 12 Jan 1736/7 **John Frost.** [WRIGHT MARR, 58]

RACHEL 3 [John 30] bp Rumbout (Presby Ch) 15 Feb 1767 (with sis Jenny). [Rumbout Presby Ch Rec]

RACHEL 4 [Daniel 3] m after 1786 **Abijah Field.** "Rachel Wright" witn to will of Jacob Frost of Cortlandt 1786 Manor. [WRIGHT/FL by Perrine; FROST GEN, 340]

RACHEL 5 [John 13] b 9 May 1777. [WRIGHT RECORDS by Stark]

RACHEL 6 [Job 6] living 4 May 1783, named in father's will. [NYCoNY PR in NYHS 32:21]

RACHEL 7 [Job 4] m **Samuel Carpenter.** [WRIGHT/OB by Perrine]

RACHEL 8 [John 9] m ---**Simpkins.** [WRIGHT/FL by Perrine]

RACHEL 9 [Robert 1] m **Samuel Haight.** [WRIGHT/FL by Perrine]

RACHEL 10 [Micaijah 1] b prob Stephentown WestCoNY 12 Feb 1789 dsp 26 Mar 1862 m 23 Feb 1825 **Isaac Candee** of Stephentown. [WRIGHT/FL by Perrine]

RACHEL 11 m Fishkill NY 29 Oct 1797 **Simon Babcock.** [Fishkill Reformed Ch Rec]

Widow RACHEL 12 of Hudson NY. Will 5 Oct 1822 (proved 16 Jul 1835) named son William (exec), daus Polly Fisk, Abigail Hotchkiss, Ester Elias. Heirs (in 1835) William Wright, Esther Ellis, Louisa wf Almerin [sp?] Ellis, William Fisk (for whom Almerin [sp?] Ellis of Stockport was guardian); Henry, Elizabeth, and William Fisk; George, William, Harriet Jane, Mary, and Elizabeth Dunbar (for whom father Collin Dunbar of Troy RensCoNY was guardian); Ann, Amelia, Jeremiah, and Addison Hotchkiss (for whom father Samuel E. Hotchkiss of Durham GreCoNY was guardian); Maria wf of Stephen Gilbert. [ColCoNY PR, G:350,351]

RACHEL 13 [Adam 3]

Rachel (---) See Widow RACHEL
Rachel (Horton) wf [Daniel 3]

RANDALL 1 [Alanson 1] b 1819.

REBECCA 1 [Caleb 1] m **John Underhill.** [WRIGHT/OB by Perrine]

REBECCA 2 [Samuel 4] b 1770 m **William Horton.** [Private record, Janett MacEntire, Preston ID (1979)]

REBECCA 3 [Joseph 10]

Rebecca (Bloom) wf [Samuel 9]
Rebecca (Buys) wf [Gabriel 1]
Rebecca (Chace) wf [Walter 2]
Rebecca (Stannard) wf [Ebenezer 1]

REUBEN 1 Beekman NY tax list Feb 1763-Jun 1765. [Beekman Tax Lists]

REUBEN 2 [John 9] b ca 1740 d Stephentown (Somers) NY 1804 m 1) **Sarah Smith** b 26 Dec

1737 d 7 Sept 1768 dau Rev John Smith m 2) 3 Nov 1769 **Phebe Quimby** dau Ephraim Quimby. Reuben and Phebe sell land in Dutchess Co (date not noted), mortgage to John Griffin 1775 (in West Patent - Northcastle). Quaker - but also said Sgt in a CT unit. Millright of Westchester in 1775. Will 4 Jun 1804 proved 8 Oct 1804. Rec Stephentown WestCoNY 1790 w/13 in fam. Acct with Dr Cornelius 22 Dec 1794 to 26 Jan 1803 names wf ch Hannah, Nathan, Phebe. Issue: James, Reuben 1778, Ephraim ?1776, Elizabeth m Jesse Hallock, Sarah 1775 m Reuben Haight, Phebe, Mary, Hannah, prob Nathan. [DutCoNY Deeds M:261, Mortg C:9; WRIGHT/FL by Perrine; WRIGHT MARR, 58; 400 YEARS by Larry Wright, 233; 1790 Census; CORNELIUS LEDGER]

REUBEN JR 3 [Reuben 2] b Stephentown WestCoNY 26 Mar 1778 d May 1843. Acct with Dr Cornelius 23 Jul 1802. [WRIGHT/FL by Perrine; CORNELIUS LEDGER]

REUBEN 4 [Adam 3] b Oyster Bay LI by 1749, named in father's will.

RHODA 1 [Daniel 5] b 1780.

RICHARD 1 [Jonathan 1] bp Flushing LI 12 Dec 1694 (adult) m **Neomy Barker** dau Samuel Barker. 10 acres from father's will. Issue unknown. ["Family of Jonathan Wright of Flushing, L.I as deduced from sources collected to date" by Mary K Witherbee (Mar 1979)]

RICHARD 2 [Samuel 10] b 20 Jan 1793 d 1871 bur Schoharie (Old Stone Fort Cem) NY m **Lydia Vincent** b 1795 d 1856. Farmer Berne NY 1850, Esperance NY 1855. Issue (from Census): Margaret, Sarah, Joshua R, Elizabeth, Henry A, Lyman, Ezra, Samuel P, Susan, Elmira. [1850 Census; SCHOHARIE CO OBITS]

RICHARD J 3 [James 20] b 1827.

RICHARD 4 [Joshua 2] b 1835.

RICHARD 5 [Richard 2]

ROBERT 1 [Isaac 1] b 1737 d Carmel NY 19 May 1818 ae 81 bur Carmel (Presb Ch) NY m 1) **Joanna Mosher** d 1788 ae 43. Perh m 2) 23 Oct 1794 **Elizabeth Lee** wid of Joseph Lee dau Richard Curry. Said to have gone to Eng ca 1780 to try to claim inheritance due from gf John Wright (who d Eng ca 1768). Perh in Capt Rogers' 5th WestCoNY Battalion 1760. Said to be Pvt in NY unit in Revolution. Perh rec Frederickstown DutCoNY 1790 w/11 in fam. In DutCoNY court 1793 re "seduction of [dau] Johannah Wright". Issue: Ebenezer 1762/3, Isaac 1764, Robert 1774, William 1781, Johanna m Edward Vermilyea, Sally m I Beyea/Bouyea, Solomon, Ruth m Joseph Hempstead, Daniel C 1797, and prob Mary/Polly m John Maybie, Rachel m Samuel Haight, perh Caleb ca 1772. [SCJ, 68; WRIGHT/FL by Perrine; Jeanne Bender notes on Robert Wright's inheritance claim; 400 YEARS by Larry Wright, 234; 1790 Census; DutCoNY Court Rec #13516]

ROBERT 2 of Croton Falls NY [Robert 1737] b 1774 d Carmel NY 19 Apr 1852 ae 78 bur Lake Mahopac Churchyard, Putnam Co NY m **Marian Cunningham** dau Shubael/Hubal & Mariam (Mosher) Cunningham and twin of Mary Ann Cunningham who m Caleb Wright [qv]. Cooper. Issue: Robert 1795, Phebe 1798, Elizabeth, 1799 m Eleazer Ferguson, John 1801, Edward 1804, Ebenezer 1807, Delilah 1810 m Smith Austin Dean, Mary Ann m Abel Gamong. [WRIGHT/FL by Perrine; "Hon Edward Wright", PUTNAM COUNTY HIST by Pelletreau, 240; WESTCHESTER COUNTY HIST by Scharf, 1:678]

ROBERT 3 d 1790, of Fredericktown, Dutchess Co NY m perh ---**Brundige**. Taxed Fredericksburgh Pct 1777. Perh rec Frederickstown DutCo NY 1790 w/3 in fam. Will 25 Mar 1790 proved 11

Oct 1790 names f/l Andrew Brundige and unnamed brothers and sisters. Only son: Nathaniel. [DutCoNY PR A:208; Fredericksburg Tax List 1777, in PUTNAM COUNTY HIST by Pelletreau, 127; 1790 Census]

ROBERT 4 d E Fishkill NY, 21 Aug 1855. Will 13 May 1854 names William (Fairfax VA), Jacob (Fishkill), Jane m Elijah B Phelps, Adilla m Nathan Smalley, Elizabeth m ---Smalley, Hiram (Po'keepsie), Robert (Fairfax VA), Sara, Jacob (Fairfax VA), Isaac R (dec'd and his chn Martha, Phebe Ann minors). [DutCoNY PR #4743, S:604]

ROBERT 5 [Robert 2] b 1795.

ROBERT 6 [Isaac 4] b 1818.

ROBERT 7 [Robert 4]. Of Fairfax VA.

ROBERT CARTER 8 [William 4]] b 1806/1810 bp Flushing (St George's Ch) LI 5 May 1810. [St George's Ch Rec

ROBERT LAY 9 [George 4] b 1786.

ROSE 1 [John 1] m 1) **Nathaniel Coles** b Oyster Bay LI 24 Aug 1668 d 8 Sept 1705 son Nathaniel & Martha (Jackson) Coles m 2) **John Townsend**. Issue: Wright 1704. [WRIGHT/OB by Perrine]

Roxana (---) wf [Laurence 1]
Roxana (Crowl) wf [Daniel 23]

RUTH 1 [Charles 1] bp Flushing (Episc Ch) 3 Mar 1727.

RUTH 2 [Isaac 1] m ---**Lee**. [WRIGHT/FL by Perrine]

RUTH 3 [John 6] b 31 Oct 1751. [WRIGHT RECORDS by Stark]

RUTH 4 [John 13] b 11 Aug 1779. [WRIGHT RECORDS by Stark]

RUTH 5 [Robert 1] m **Joseph Hempstead.** [WRIGHT/FL by Perrine]

RUTH 6 [John 16] No record. [DUTCHESS COUNTY HIST, 498]

RUTH 7 [William 2] b 1775.

RUTH 8 [William 14]

Ruth (Bailey) wf [John 6]
Ruth (Lee) wf [Isaac 1]
Ruth (Miller) wf [Micaijah 1]

S

SALLY See also SARAH.

SALLY 1 [Robert 1737] perh m ---**Lee** by 14 Apr 1803 perh m **I Beyea/Bouyea**. "Sally Lee dau Robert Wright" in Dr Cornelius' Ledger. [WRIGHT/FL by Perrine; CORNELIUS LEDGER]

SALLY 2 [Jotham 3] b 1787.

SALLY 3 [Jacob 11]

SALLY 4 [Matthew 1]

SALLY 5 [William 23]

SALLY ANN 6 [David 10]

SAMUEL 1 [Jonathan 1] perh m Newtown (Presby Ch) LI **Mrs. Sarah Morrel** perh 2nd wife. Got 20 acres from father's will. Prob to Newtown LI and had land (he lived on but evidently didn't own) beq 15 Jan 1715/16 to Jonathan Hunt by will of his father Edward Hunt. Issue (bp Newtown (Presby Ch) LI): Grace 1738, Deborah 1738, and perh Gabriel. [WRIGHT/FL by Perrine; Newtown Presby Ch Rec]

SAMUEL 2 [Gabriel 1] bp Fishkill NY 25 Jun 1736 (spons Abraham Buys & Ragel Terbos). Prob Beekman Tax List Feb-Jun 1756. [Fishkill Reformed Ch Rec; Beekman Tax Lists]

SAMUEL 3 b 13 Mar 1740 bur Flushing (St George's Ch) LI 28 Aug 1815 m by 1775 **Elizabeth---** b 3 Sep 1752 both bp Flushing (St George's Ch) LI 5 Aug 1798, with chn. Issue:

William 1775, Catherine 1782, Lydia 1784, Hannah 1790. [St George's Ch Rec in RECORD, 112:42]

SAMUEL B 4 b perh Holland say 1740/45 d Caesar, Dearborn Co IN 29 Dec 1831 m **Catherine Fox** b perh Holland ca 1747 d Caesar IN betw 1820/23. Trad from Holland. Of Utica ca 1770-74. Perh res Whitestown, MontCoNY 1790 (Gabriel Wright [qv] in same town 1790). Of Rome, OneidaCoNY 1800, OntCoNY 1810, Indiana 1814/18. See Samuel 2. Issue: Rebecca 1770 m William Horton, Naomi ca 1772 m Moses Hull, Jonathan 1774, Peter Bice 1776, Nathaniel 1778, William 1780, Hannah 1782, Elizabeth 1786, Eunice 1788, Thomas 1790. [*Ancestry and Descendants of Jonathan Calkins Wright, 1766-1958* by Estel L. Wright (1958); Mary K Witherbee notes; private records of Jannett McEntire, Preston ID]

SAMUEL 5 d 31 Dec 1754 m **Martha Knowels** d 1 Jan 1755. Issue: Jonathan 1745. [Bible Rec from Charlene F Bryan, Sherburne NY.]

SAMUEL 6 b 12 May 1754 d 7 Jul 1811 m **Susan London**. Pvt NY in Rev. [DAR Patriots Index, Vol 2]

SAMUEL 7 [David 3] b perh Hempstead NY 4 Mar 1756 d Hempstead (bur Presby Ch) NY 8 Mar 1835 ae 79 m **Martha [? Davenport]** d 10 June 1838 ae 72 perh dau Lewis & Martha Davenport. Issue (b 1790/97): Nathaniel 1797, 3 daus, 1 other son. [WRIGHTS OF LONG ISLAND by Francis Wright]

SAMUEL 8 b 7 Aug 1753 d Salem NY 3 Apr 1837 m **Sarah———**. Pvt DutCoNY. Partial issue: Samuel m Hannah Welsh. [DAR Patriots Index; DAR Lineage Bk 40:330, 42:108]

SAMUEL 9 m (License) 21 Nov 1759 **Rebecca Bloom**. [WRIGHT MARR, 59]

SAMUEL 10 b 17 Jun 1757 d Berne NY 19 Jan 1831 ae 73-6-26 bur So Berne (Wright Burying Ground) m Rhinebeck (RDC) NY 18 Dec 1776 **Margaret Wilsey** b 19 Jul 1755 d Berne NY 22 Aug 1839 ae 84-1-3. Perh "Samuel Jr" of Nine Partners 1778-79 Tax List. Clinton Tax List (not in 1787). Yeoman of Clinton NY 1790, Berne 1800. Bo't Lot 544 Manor of Rensselaerwyck, Berne ca 1808. Will 4 Jan 1831. Issue: Elizabeth 1779 m Thomas Hayes, Abigail 1781 m Godfrey Radner, John S 1783, Lydia 1785 m Gabriel Barton, James J 1787, Phebe 1788 m Joseph Wright, Laurence 1790, Richard 1793, Polly/Mary 1797. ["Wright Family Record," in National Genealogical Society *Quarterly* 61:145; AlbCoNY PR 8:82; Rhinebeck RDC Rec; 1790 & 1800 Census; CRUM ELBOW TAX LISTS]

SAMUEL 11 [John 13] b 9 Dec 1768. [WRIGHT RECORDS by Stark]

SAMUEL S 12 of Berne NY, b ca 1778 d Berne NY 1 Apr 1844 ae 66. [Beaver Dam RDC Rec]

SAMUEL 13 [Jotham 2] b NYC 27 Aug 1761 d NYC 5 Jul 1806 m NYC 1786 **Phebe Cheesman.** Mustered ae 17 in Aaron Aorson's Co Col Peter Gansevoort's NY Reg't. Military Pension. Exec for est of bro/law Joseph Cheesman 1800. Issue: Sarah 1787 m James Oliver, Joseph Cheesman 1790, Mary 1792, Sarah (2nd) 1795, Harriet 1797, Charles Sammis 1800, Susan 1804. [Military Pension #W18461; DAR Lineage Bk 17:138,139; NYCoNY PR 43:315 (Joseph Cheesman) in NYHS 39:239; WRIGHT/OB by Perrine]

SAMUEL 14 m **Catherine Thornton.** Issue (bp Schenectady 1st Reformed Ch): David 1795. [IGI 84]

SAMUEL 15 [Daniel 16] b 28 Mar 1763 3 31 Jul 1827 m **Mary Putney** of Amawalk NY. [WRIGHT/OB by Perrine]

SAMUEL 16 [Thomas 11] b Coxsackie NY 14 Sept 1799 bp 1799 Coxsackie RDC. [Coxsackie RDC Rec]

SAMUEL 17 [William 4] b 1806/1810 bp Flushing (St George's Ch) LI 5 May 1810. [St George's Ch Rec, in RECORD, 112:45]

SAMUEL 18 [Richard 2] b 1832.

SAMUEL 19 son [William 24]

SAMUEL J 20 [James 20] b 1814.

SAMUEL PURDY 21 [Charles 5]

SAMUEL WASHBURN 22 [William 2] b 1789.

SANFORD 1 [Alanson 1]

SARAH See also SALLY.

SARAH 1 [Nicholas 2] b by 1674 m **Josiah Latting**. [WRIGHT/OB by Perrine]

SARAH 2 [? Henry 1] m Hempstead (Grace Ch) LI 6 Oct 1715 **Abraham Everett**. [GRACE CH by Ladd, 281]

SARAH 3 [Edmund 1] m **Samuel Birdsall**. [WRIGHT/OB by Perrine; "Birdsall Bible Record," in RECORD (1934), 61:121]

SARAH 4 [John 2] m ---**Lee**. [WRIGHT/FL by Perrine]

SARAH 5 [William 3] m (License) 24 Jul 1737 **John Townsend**. [WRIGHT MARR, 59]

SARAH 6 [Jonathan 2] unm 1744. [WRIGHT/FL by Perrine]

SARAH 7 [Daniel 3] m 1) **Jacob Frost** son Samuel & Keziah (Wright) Frost m 2) Amawalk NY (per

Quaker Records) 16 Jan 1805 **Daniel Carpenter** of Stephentown NY. Res Peekskill NY. His will proved 27 May 1786. Issue: Daniel Wright, Anne 1776, Elizabeth, Rachel. [WRIGHT/FL by Perrine; FROST GEN, 339]

SARAH 8 m perh Fishkill NY ca 1757 **William Horton** b Fishkill NY ca 1737 son John & Elizabeth (Lee) Horton. 8 chn b Fishkill. [HORTON GEN, 13]

SARAH 9 [Benjamin 3] m (License) 26 Jun 1773 **Samuel Carman.** [WRIGHT/OB by Perrine; WRIGHT MARR, 59]

SARAH 10 [David 5] perh m **Capt Charles Halstead** (per DAR Rec). But see this: Capt Charles Halstead (son of Gershom) b 3 Sep 1789 d 29 Jun 1860 m 1) Charlotte Smith d Newburgh NY 1834 m 2) her sister Tabitha Smith. [DAR Lineage Book 119:60; "Halstead Corrections," in RECORD, 90:244; WRIGHT OF LONG ISLAND, by Francis Wright, 14]

SARAH 11 m (License) 6 Sept 1764 **Samuel Hallett.** [WRIGHT MARR, 59]

SARAH 12 [Thomas 2] named in will of gf Joseph Cooper Aug 1778 as "dau of Thomas Wright Doctor". [NYCoNY PR 27:364 in NYHS 37:83]

SARAH 13 [Jacob 2] b Somers NY 1757 (or 1 Oct 1747 per Perrine) d Po'keepsie NY 7 Oct 1807 (or 10 Oct 1801 per Perrine) m Crum Elbow, DutCoNY 1769 **Thomas Nelson** b 17 Mar 1744 d Po'keepsie NY 1 Nov 1823 son John & Elizabeth Nelson. He m 2) Mrs Mary (Thompson) Delavan. [*Thomas Davenport and His Descendants* by Dorothea Giles and Irma Franklin, 211; WRIGHT/FL by Perrine; WRIGHT MARR, 59]

SARAH 14 [William 5] m **John Townsend.** [WRIGHT/OB by Perrine]

SARAH 15 [James 4] b perh New Castle NY 22 Jan 1757 m **Thomas Hawxhurst.** [WRIGHT/OB by Perrine]

SARAH 16 [Jotham 2] m **Joseph Latham.** [WRIGHT/OB by Perrine]

SARAH 17 m (License) 18 Dec 1782 **Terance Reilly.** [WRIGHT MARR, 59]

SARAH 18 [Job 6] living 4 May 1783, named in father's will.

SARAH 19 [Reuben 2] b 25 Feb 1775 d 25 Mar 1853 m 14 Aug 1793 **Reuben Haight** b 5 Aug 1769 son James & Bathsheba Haight of North Castle. Hatter and farmer of Shappagua NY, later Canada West. Hicksite Quaker. 12 ch. [WRIGHT/FL by Perrine; HAIGHT GEN by Hoyt, 541]

SARAH 20 [Daniel 20] b 1 Aug 1802 bp Hackensack [Reform DC] NY 21 Jul 1802. [New Hackensack RDC Rec]

SARAH 21 [Abijah 1] living 1812, named in will of gf Benjamin Wright. [WRIGHT/FL by Perrine]

SARAH 22 [Uriah 1] bp 1761.

SARAH 23 [Samuel 13] b NYC 1795.

SARAH 24 [Isaac 2] m Dutchess Co NY 20 Jul 1814 **Daniel Doane.** [WRIGHT/FL by Perrine]

SARAH 25 [Richard 2] b 1814.

SARAH 26 [Adam 4]

SARAH 27 [Alanson 1] b 1825

SARAH 28 [Caleb 4]

SARAH 29 [Benjamin 3]

SARAH 30 [Robert 4] of East Fishkill

SARAH ANN 31 [Abraham 6] of Fishkill

SARAH J 32 [William 13] b 1823.

SARAH M 33 [Abraham 7] of Pleasant Valley

SARAH M 34 [Isaac 2] of Fishkill

SARAH 35 [Hiram 2]

Sally (Williams) wf [Isaac 7]
Sally Ann (Frost) wf [John 42]
Sarah (----) wf [Job 6]
Sarah (----) wf [John 9]
Sarah (----) wf [William 3]
Sarah (----) wf [William 23]
Sarah (----) wf [John 2]
Sarah (Babcock) wf [Abraham 3]
Sarah (Bouck) wf [John 44]
Sarah (Colwell) wf [William 25]
Sarah (Hall) wf [James 15]
Sarah (Hull) wf [James 18]
Sarah (Huyck) wf [Thomas 1]
Sarah (Ludlam) wf [John 5]
Sarah (Magra) wf [Mark 1]
Sarah (Mede) wf [Joseph 12]
Sarah (Mekell) wf [Charles 4]
Sarah (Morrel) wf [Samuel 1]
Sarah (Pladdo) wf [William 12]
Sarah (Read) wf [Edward 1]
Sarah (Saitley) wf [Jonathan 1]
Sarah (Shed) wf [Nathaniel 4]
Sarah (Smith) wf [Reuben 2]
Sarah (VanWyck) wf [John 27]
Sarah (Walters) wf [Daniel 16]
Sarah (Wells) wf [Thomas 6]
Sarah (Wilcox) wf [Alanson 1]

SILAS 1 [David 3]

SILAS 2 [John 46] b 1812.

SIMEON 1 Nine Partners NY Tax list Feb 1753-Jun 1756 and Feb 1759-Feb 1762. [CRUM ELBOW TAX LISTS]

SIMEON 2 of Dutchess Co NY deeds to Martin Hoffman 1757. [DutCoNY Deeds 3:56,57]

SIMEON 3 of Amenia NY, mortgaged Lot 63 in Oblong, Amenia NY 112 acres, 10 Nov 1763. Overseer of the poor 16 Jul 1768. Amenia NY tax list Jun 1762-1770, mortgages 1763. "Cymeon" of Amenia in DutCoNY court recs 1767-70. Said to have settled DutCoNY ca 1740 and at Rutland VT 1771. [DutCoNY Mort 1:299; "Amenia Precinct Book of the Poor 1768-1817", in *The Dutchess* Sept 1975; DutCoNY Court Rec #4936, 6954, 6858, 6998; Query 394 in NEHGS *NEXUS*, 1:68]

SIMEON/SYMON 4 of WestCoNY, pvt in William Willett's co North Battalion 1760. [NY Muster Rolls, in NYHS Vol 24]

SIMEON 5 [Jacob 2] m prob Yorktown NY **Esther Horton** dau Daniel & Esther (Lane) Horton. Issue: Simon 1775. [SCJ, 339; WRIGHT/FL by Perrine]

SIMON 1 [Simeon 5] b prob Yorktown NY 14 Feb 1775 d 30 Jan 1861 bur Peekskill (VanCortlandt Cem) NY m 1) Cortlandt NY 31 Dec 1799 **Mary Fowler** b 14 Feb 1779 d 12 Feb 1804 dau Joseph & Sarah (Whitney) Fowler m 2) 11 Nov 1807 **Elizabeth Barton** b 16 Aug 1775 d 11 Jun 1837 dau Caleb Barton and sis of Gabriel Barton who m 1802 Lydia Wright [qv]. Issue: Joseph Fowler 1800, James 1802, Mary 1804, Eliza 1804 (twin) d young, Lewis Barton 1809, Anna Maria 1815, Phoebe 1817, George 1825. [WRIGHT/FL by Perrine; SCJ, 352, 380; BARTON GEN by McCracken]

SIMON 2 [Gilbert 5] b 1835.

SOLOMON 1 weaver, b Queens Co NY ca 1740. Enlisted in Capt Jesse Platt's Suffolk Co Militia 28 Apr 1760 (age 20). [NY Muster Rolls in NYHS Vol 24]

SOLOMON 2 [Adam 3] m (License) 26 Aug 1768 **Mary Hawkhurst** dau Samson & Jerusha (Smith) Hawxhurst of North Hempstead. Of Carmel NY. Perh rec Fishkill DutCoNY 1790 w/7 in fam. Issue: Solomon. [SCJ, 356; 1790 Census; WRIGHT/OB by Perrine; WRIGHT MARR, 59]

SOLOMON 3 [Solomon 2] m WestCoNY 18 Jan 1801 (by Silas Constant) **Zilpha Baldwin** dau Elisha & Elizabeth (Cromwell) Baldwin. To Elgin IL ca 1836. Issue: Baldwin, Elizabeth m Gilbert Wright [5], Mary Emeline, Elisha Cromwell, William. [SCJ, 356; WRIGHT/OB by Perrine]

SOLOMON 4 [Robert 1] of WestCoNY m 2 Mar 1803 ———. [SCJ, 381]

SOLOMON 5 Dutchess Co NY, bo't of Joseph Huntley 1796. [DutCoNY Mortg 7:65,66]

Sophia (Platt) wf HIRAM 1

STEPHEN 1 of Nine Partners NY, witnessed deeds betw John Rogers to Stephen Nelson 29 June 1782 and to Reuben Nelson of Charlotte 16 Jun 1785. [DutCoNY Deeds 31:1, 14:323]

STEPHEN 2 [Thomas 18] b 25 Nov 1770 d 24 Nov 1834 m 1) East Chester NY 1795 **Elizabeth Wright** m 2) **Martha Dodge** of Jericho LI. Res Division St NYC. Issue: Edwin 1796, William 1800, Stephen 1802, John 1805, Daniel Dodge 1809. [WRIGHT/OB by Perrine: NYCoNY PR 95:56, Adm 33:83; WRIGHT MARR, 59]

STEPHEN 3 of Albany Co NY, b by 1765 living 1820, rec Clinton NY 1790, Berne NY 1800, 1820; bo't of Daniel Wright W 1/2 of Lot 542 Rensselaerwyck, Berne 1802. [AlbCoNY Deeds

186:495]

STEPHEN THORN 4 [Caleb 4] b Carmel NY 19 Jan 1811 d South East NY 27 Apr 1873 bur Carmel (Union Valley Ch Cem) m Carmel NY **Dorinda Merrick** dau Ezra & Eliza Merrick. Issue: Caleb 1833, Ezra 1835, Stephen 1838, David 1840, Mary 1842. [WRIGHT/OB by Perrine, 195]

STEPHEN 5 b WestCoNY ca 1768 d Lower Bedeque PEI 19 Jan 1841 m Tryon PEI Jul 1791 **Frances Lord** b Tryon PEI ca 1771 d Lower Bedeque PEI 4 Feb 1863. See source for issue and extended lineage. See NATHANIEL 9. [LOYALIST CLAIMS, 770]

STEPHEN 6 [Stephen 2] b 1802.

STEPHEN 7 [Stephen 4] b 1838.

SUSAN 1 [Samuel 13] b 1804.

SUSAN 2 m Poughkeepsie NY 17 May 1829 **William F Williams**. [IGI 84]

SUSAN 3 [Gilbert 5] b 1830.

SUSAN 4 [Benjamin 4]

SUSAN 5 [Gideon 4]

SUSAN 6 [Richard 2]

SUSAN ANN 7 [Lewis 1] b 1834.

Susan (Bassett) wf [John 35]
Susan (Briggs) wf [Ebenezer 6]
Susan (Brinkerhoff) wf [Abraham 6]
Susan (London) wf [Samuel 6]

SUSANNA 1 [Jonathan 2] bp Jamaica (RDC) 26 Apr 1709 unm 1768. [WRIGHT/FL by Perrine]

SUSANNA 2 [William 2] b 1767.

Widow SUSANNA 3 of WestCoNY. Husb (---) WRIGHT d St John's NB 27 Feb 1785. He said in Loyal Militia from 1779 "until he was disbanded" in NY. Widow's Loyalist claim rejected. See source for more detail. [*American Loyalist Claims, Vol 1*, abstracted from the Public Records Office, Audit Office Series 13, Bundles 1-35 & 37, by Peter Wilson Coldham. Washington DC: National Genealogical Society (1980), p 540]

SUSANNA 4 aka Sukey [John 22] b 27 Feb 1782 bp Berne (Beaver Dam RDC) NY 13 Sep 1801 m **Matthias/Matthew Strevel**, and had issue (b Berne NY): Harvy 1800, Isaac 1802. [St Paul's Evang Luth Ch Rec; Beaver Dam RDC Berne NY Rec; Private record, Joe V Wright, Haverford PA (1979)]

SUSANNAH 5 [William 8] b 1784.

SUSANNA 6 [John 26] b 1789.

SUSANNA 7 [Isaac 4] b 1828.

SUSANNA 8 dau [Jacob 1]

Susanna (Palmer) wf [Charles 3]
Susanna (Stephens) wf [Dennis 2]

SYDNEY 1 [Alanson 1] b 1820.

SYLVANUS 1 [Charles 4] b prob Philipstown NY 1797. No further record. [WRIGHT/FL by Perrine]

SYLVANUS 2 [Gideon 1] liv Mar 1736 m **Mary Proctor**. Of Mill Neck LI. Issue: Charles. [WRIGHT/OB by Perrine]

SYLVESTER 1 [John 47]

T

TABITHA 1 [Anthony 2] b perh Staten Island m by 1739 ---**Randall**. "Jacob Phitz Randall" (? Fitz Randolph) co-exec 1746 of Anthony Wright's 1739 will. Perrine says he was ---Bondet. [NYCoNY PR 16:58 (Anthony Wright) in NYHS 28:105; WRIGHT/OB by Perrine]

Tabitha (Sammis) wf [Jotham 2]

TEMPERANCE 1 [George 4] b 1764.

Temperance (Kirk) wf [Joseph 1]
Temperance (Reader) wf [David 6]

THEDA 1 [Gilbert 5] b 1840.

THEODORE A 1 [Enos 1]

THEODORE 2 [Gilbert 5] b 1838.

THOMAS 1 m (License) 28 Aug 1696 **Lydia Cobbit**. [WRIGHT MARR, 60]

THOMAS 2 [Edmund 2] b Oyster Bay by 1731 m 1) **Elizabeth A Cooper** d 12 Jan 1755 dau Joseph Cooper m 2) (License) 22 Nov 1755 **Elizabeth Rochell** dau Johannes & Anna (Bajeau) Grosbeck. Physician of Eastchester NY as late as 15 Oct 1768. Adm 7 Aug 1786 to son John Wright physician and s/l William Wright. Said prisoner in the Provost, NYC, in Revolution. Issue: Sarah, John Grosbeck, Elizabeth. [Query by William W Conway in RECORD (1897), 28:117 which has Stephen [2] as a son by an unknown 3rd wife; NYCoNY Adm in NYHS 38:343; WRIGHT/OB by Perrine; WRIGHT MARR, 60]

THOMAS 3 b Goshen OraCoNY ca 1739. Enlisted in Capt Howell's OraCo Militia 3 Apr 1760 (b OraCo age 21 5'10"), perh same in Capt Benjamin Stevens' WestCo Militia 20 June 1762 (b OraCo age 21 5'10"). [NY Muster Rolls in NYHS Vol 24]

THOMAS 4 b Ireland ca 1737 liv WestCoNY 4 May 1760, when he enlisted in Capt Jonathan Haight's WestCo Militia (age 23). [NY Muster Rolls in NYHS Vol 24]

THOMAS 5 yeoman of Orange Co NY d by 13 Jun 1758. Adm to Robert Thompson, principle creditor. [Adm in NYHS 29:434, also ALBANY WILLS, 416]

THOMAS 6 m (License) 28 Oct 1758 **Sarah Wells**. [WRIGHT MARR, 60]

THOMAS 7 m (License) 9 Nov 1761 **Mary McQuirrey**. [WRIGHT MARR, 60]

THOMAS 8 [William 1] b Philipstown NY d LaGrange NY living 29 Dec 1809 (named in will of gf) m **Elizabeth Crane** dau Nathaniel & Martha (Townsend) Crane of Carmel NY. Res LaGrange, DutCoNY. Issue: Lewis 1801, 7 others. [WRIGHT/FL by Perrine; DutCoNY PR, D:125]

THOMAS 9 of Dutchess Co NY m b 23 Aug 1782 **Elizabeth Banker**. Perh rec Fishkill DutCoNY 1790 w/5 in fam. Issue (bp Hopewell NY): Daniel 1782. [Hopewell RDC Rec; Fishkill RDC Rec; 1790 Census]

THOMAS 10 [Daniel 5] b 1785 d 1867 m 1812 **Naomi Young**. [DAR Lineage Bk 76:73]

THOMAS 11 of Coxsackie NY m **Sarah Huyck**. Issue (bp Coxsackie RDC): Samuel 1799, Polly 1804. [Coxsackie RDC Rec; IGI 84]

THOMAS 12 [Samuel 4] b perh Rome NY 1790 m **Electa Shed.** [Private record of Jannett MacEntire, Preston ID]

THOMAS 13 m Port Richmond, Staten Island NY 18 Mar 1798 **Catherine Blake.** [WRIGHT MARR, 60]

THOMAS 14 of Albany NY ?, b ca 1796, d 16 Dec 1846 ae 50, "of the firm of Relyea & Wright". [Munsell's *Annals of Albany*, Vol 10]

THOMAS 15 [Charles 4] b perh Philipstown NY 28 Feb 1800 d 27 Aug 1854. [WRIGHT/FL by Perrine]

THOMAS 16 [Jacob 10] bp Cobleskill (Zions Evangel Ch) NY 22 Apr 1810. [IGI 84]

THOMAS 17 of Fishkill m by 15 Mar 1811 **Margaret---**, when they mortgaged in Fishkill. [DutCoNY Mortg 16:52]

THOMAS 18 [Adam 3] d 8 Jul 1786 m **Mary---**. Of North Castle WestCoNY. Unrecorded will 1 Dec 1776 names Benjamin Hildreth Jr & Thomas Griswold exec. Miller and a Quaker. Said [by McCann] to have settled at Compasture River VA 1746 with bro Peter. Issue: Sarah, Elizabeth, Stephen, Thomas. [WRIGHT/OB by Perrine; NYHS 36:195,207; *Ancestors-Descendants of James Wilson Wright Sr...* by W.R. & R.L. McCann (1954), 5]

THOMAS [Isaac 4] b 1812.

THOMAS [Lewis 1] b 1833.

THOMAS son [Matthew 1]

Tirza (Chapin) wf [Caleb 6]
Tryphena (Tracy) wf [Jonathan 6]

U V W

URIAH 1 [Dennis 1] m (License) 26 Aug 1760 **Margaret Williams.** Res Huntington LI. Issue: Sarah bp 1761. [WRIGHT/OB by Perrine; RECORD 11:49; WRIGHT MARR, 60]

URIAH 2 of Fredericksburg Pct d by 1777 when estate taxed. [Fredericksburg Pct Tax List 1777, in PUTNAM COUNTY HIST by Pelletreau, 127]

URIAH 3 [Charles 4] b 1795 d by 1830. Not in father's 1830 will. [WRIGHT/FL by Perrine]

WALTER 1 b Queens Co NY ca 1781 liv Richmondville Schoharie Co NY 1855 aged 74 with son Daniel. Issue: Daniel ca 1805, prob Demosthenes, Walter Jr, Elijah. [1855 NY State Census]

WALTER 2 [Daniel 17] m Pleasant Valley [Presby Ch] NY 16 Feb 1802 **Rebecca Chace.** [POUGHKEEPSIE M&D by Reynolds; PV Presby Ch Rec]

WALTER JR 3 [Walter 1] Prob rec Carlisle SchCoNY 1835. With bro Demosthenes & Elijah mortg land in Richmondville SchCoNY 1850 and buys of Daniel Wright there 1851. Walter Jr & wf sell to Elijah & Demosthenes 1854. [SchCoNY Deeds 21:441, 28:259, Mortg W:179, 1835 NY State Census]

WALTER 4 b Ettrick Forest, Scotland, ca 1763 d Fishkill NY 29 Jun 1840 bur Fishkill RDC. [FISHKILL TOMBSTONES]

WALTER [Daniel 21] b 1833.

WALTER [William 23]

WEALTHY 1 [Ambrose 1] b 1803.

WEBSTER [George 7]

Wilhelmina (---) wf [Daniel 21]

WILLIAM 1 [John 9] b prob Flushing LI Jan 1736 d Philipstown NY 22 Jan 1812 m 1760/70 **Jemima Haight** b 18 Sep 1739 d 9 Dec 1825 dau Daniel Haight. Will 26 Dec 1809 proved 3 Jul 1812 names ch and grandsons William and Jacob. Perh rec Philipstown WestCoNY 1790 w/6 in fam. Issue: Caleb 1755, Charles 1762, Mary m ---Beaumont, Ann/Nancy m 1) Isaac or Zebulon Mead m 2) ---Horton, Joseph, Enos 1772, Thomas. [WRIGHT/FL by Perrine; DutCoNY PR D:125; Query 5160-3 in *Connecticut Nutmegger* 11:474; IGI NY 1984; 1790 Census]

WILLIAM 2 [John 6] b perh Oyster Bay LI 20 Aug 1744 m perh ---**Washburn**. Res Putnam Co NY. Acct with Dr Cornelius 15 May 1787 to 31 Dec 1803 says "asset to him in Isaac Lounsberry Sr's account." Issue: Susanna 1767 m Isaac Lownsberry, Deborah P 1768, Barnabas 1769, Ruth 1775 m George Remsen, Zebulon 1776, John 1778 (of Brooklyn NY), Mary 1780, William Jr 1782, Ann 1784 m David Dean, Matilda 1787, Samuel Washburn 1789 (of Passaic NJ). [NYS DAR Rec 23:184; WRIGHT RECORDS by Stark, 161]

WILLIAM 3 [? John 18] b North Castle WestCoNY 10 Jan 1753 m **Sarah Lyons**. Lieut in Capt Jacobus Purdy's Co, Col Thomas' 2nd WestCoNY Reg't. Perh "William of North Castle" who with wf Sarah mortg to George Townsend of Oyster Bay 1789 and again Sep 1790. Prob rec North Castle WestCoNY 1790 w/9 in fam. See William 23. Issue (partial): James 1787. [DAR Lineage Book 118:175; DutCoNY Mortg D:103,398; 1790 Census]

WILLIAM 4 [Samuel 3] b 27 Oct 1775 bp Flushing (St George's Ch) LI 5 Aug 1798 m by 1794 **Jane---** liv 25 Feb 1834. Issue: Jane 1794, Ann Bell 1798, Margaret 1806, Fanny L m George Wallace Birck, Samuel, Robert Carter, William, Jane Bell m John J Jones. [St George's Ch Rec, in RECORD, 112:42,44,45]

WILLIAM 5 [Caleb 1] b Oyster Bay 8 Dec 1680 d 9 Nov 1759 m 1706 **Elizabeth Rhodes** dau John & Diana Rhodes. Issue: John 1707, Ann m William Crooker, Elizabeth, Mary m Joseph Cooper, Sarah m John Townsend, Elizabeth (2nd), Caleb 1739.

WILLIAM 6 m (License) 15 Sep 1781 **Zipporah Coals** prob dau Joseph & Charity (Valentine) Coles. ["Anne Mott" by Hopper S Mott, in RECORD (1905), 36:60,61; WRIGHT MARR, 60]

WILLIAM 7 m (License) 25 May 1782 **Margaret Henry.** Issue (bp NYC Presby Ch): Elizabeth 1785. [WRIGHT MARR, 60; 1st/2nd Presby Ch Rec]

WILLIAM 8 [John 15] b Oyster Bay 21 Oct 1748 d 11 Mar 1820 m prob East Chester NY (License) 6 Feb 1783 **Elizabeth Wright** dau Dr Thomas & Elizabeth (Grosbeck) Wright of East Chester. Of Pelham Manor co-adm of f/l Dr Thomas Wright's est. Issue: Susannah 1784, Caleb 1787, Nancy 1790, Mary 1799. [WRIGHT/OB by Perrine; WRIGHT MARR, 60]

WILLIAM 9 of NY, deeds 100 acres in Stephentown, Albany Co NY [E side of Hudson], to Theodore Boardman 8 Jul 1771. [AlbCoNY Deeds 8:457]

WILLIAM 10 of Nine Partners NY, leased Lot 523 Manor of Rensselaerwyck, Berne NY 11 May 1795. Rec Berne NY 1800 (William "Right"), 1810, 1820. Possible issue: David 1801. [AlbCoNY Deeds 186:495]

WILLIAM 11 [Benjamin 3] prob the butcher who m NYC (1st/2nd Presby Ch) 15 Mar 1788 **Margaret Marsh**. Perh same who was a Quaker and assessed NYC (Ward 2) 1812-15. See also ALLISON prob his brother. [WRIGHT MARRIAGES; "Returns of Quakers in New York City... 1810-1819" by B-Ann Morehouse, in RECORD, 110:165]

WILLIAM 12 of Albany, m 11 Jun 1764 **Sara Pladdo**. [Albany (RDC) NY Rec 1926-1927]

WILLIAM 13 [Robert 1] b 10 Jan 1781 d Mahopac NY 10 Nov 1858 ae 77 bur Mahopac (Meth Ch) NY m Dutchess Co NY 2 Mar 1803 **Margaret/Margery Sloat** d 19 Jan 1841 ae 62 bur Mahopac Cem. Issue: James 1814, Marcus, Platt S 1821, Harrison, Delilah 1827, Johannah m Elijah Craft, Sarah J 1823. [POUGHKEEPSIE M&D by Reynolds; WRIGHT/FL by Perrine; PUTNAM COUNTY by Pelletreau]

WILLIAM 14 [William 2] of Ovid NY, b Dutchess (now Putnam Co) NY 1782 , d Ovid, Seneca Co NY, m **Jane Blain** b Warwick NY 12 Oct 1782 d Galensburg MI 3 Jul 1867. Issue: Anna m Peter Limmer (of Gallopsville NY), John Lownsberry, Ruth m ---Whitaker, Susanna m ---Stratton, Ira, Lydia m Daniel Holden, Isaac, Letson, Wright, Mary m ---Bentley, William, Enos, Elizabeth, Catherine. [NYS DAR Rec 23:184]

WILLIAM 15 [Adam 4] b perh Hempstead LI 1757 d 1822. [WRIGHT/OB by Perrine]

WILLIAM 16 [Job 6], living 4 May 1783, named in fathers will.

WILLIAM F 17 [Jacob 7] b say 1760 bp Rumbout (St George's Ch, Hempstead) NY 14 Jun 1762 with f and other chn. [St George's Ch Rec in RECORD, 11:49]

WILLIAM 18 [Joseph 12] b 17 Jan 1783 bp Fishkill (Reformed Ch) 23 Feb 1790, living 26

Dec 1809. [Fishkill Reformed Ch Rec; DutCoNY PR D:125]

WILLIAM 20 [William 4] b 1806/1810 bp Flushing (St George's Ch) LI 5 May 1810. [St George's Ch Rec, in RECORD 112:45]

WILLIAM 21 [Charles 4] b perh Philipstown NY 5 Dec 1808 d 3 Nov 1882. [WRIGHT/FL by Perrine]

WILLIAM 22 of Fishkill NY m Kent CT 25 Dec 1825 **Catherine Phelps** d Dutchess Co NY 13 Sep 1835 ae 31-2-21 bur Shenandoah (Bapt Ch) Cem dau William R Phelps "of Conn.". Issue: Albert 1838 d young. ["Caroline Wright," in CEM INSC by Frost; d notice of "Catherine Wright" 23 Sep 1835, in POUGHKEEPSIE M&D by Reynolds; Kent CT VR (where is "Catherine Phelps"]

WILLIAM 23 of Coxsackie NY, m **Sarah---**, and d by 14 Sep 1840 (will proved). Perh rec Coxsackie AlbCoNY 1790 w/8 in fam. Both deeded land in Newcastle WestCoNY 1792. Of Newcastle 16 Jul 1792, mortg land in Coxsackie (Coeymans Patent) AlbCoNY conveyed by Isaac Oberpath of Coxsackie. See WILLIAM 3. Issue (from will): Thomas (Mich.), Walter (Onondaga Co NY), James (Mich.), Isaac (Onondaga Co NY), Betsey m Amos Bailey (Bethlehem NY), Sally m Eli Stan[?], William Jr (dec'd) and his son Bridgman (Syracuse NY). [GreCoNY PR 480-10640, D:166; 1790 Census; WestCoNY Deeds K:344; AlbCoNY Mortg 9:190]

WILLIAM 24 d Po'keepsie NY 15 Sep 1882, naming wf **Isabella---**, and prob issue: Margaret m ---Dunwoody, George (and his ch Sarah Ann), Gloria Ann, William, Eliza Ann, Minnie, Samuel, Mary Jane (wf John Wright dec'd and her ch William, George, Eliza). [DutCoNY PR #10274]

WILLIAM J 25 [John 22] b prob DutCoNY ca 1792 living 1850, m **Sarah Colwell**. Farmer of Berne,

Albany Co NY 1850. Sold E 1/2 of Lot 501 Berne to Joseph Wright 1844. Issue (from 1850 Census): Oscar, Amanda m Van Buren Nelson. [AlbCoNY Deeds 90:357]

WILLIAM M 26 d East Fishkill NY 22 Aup 1876, naming paternal aunts Surah Burrell, Diana Wright, and issue (minors): Martha, Freeman S. [DutCoNY PR #8600]

WILLIAM 27 of Philipse Pct 1777. [Philipse Pct Tax List 1777, PUTNAM COUNTY HIST by Pelletreau, 127]

WILLIAM 28 d Halfmoon, Saratoga Co NY by 12 Apr 1824 when adm granted to Keziah Wright, George Wright, and Benjamin Wright, all of Halfmoon. [Saratoga Co NY PR #001-13, 1:154]

WILLIAM 29 m (License) 27 Oct 1761 **Mary Jones.** [WRIGHT MARR, 60]

WILLIAM 30 m NYC 13 Nov 1776 **Mary Powers.** [WRIGHT MARR, 60]

WILLIAM JR 31 [William 2] b 1782.

WILLIAM 32 [Rev Daniel 22] Methodist Preacher

WILLIAM 33 [Samuel 4] b 1782.

WILLIAM 34 [Stephen 2] b NYC 1800.

WILLIAM 35 [Isaac 6] b 1828.

WILLIAM 36 [Solomon 3] of Westchester Co

WILLIAM 37 [William 14] of Ovid

WILLIAM 38 [Widow Rachel]

WILLIAM JR 39 [William 23] of Coxsackie

WILLIAM BRADFORD 40 [Wise 2] b 1813.

WILLIAM D 41 [David 10] b 1833.

WILLIAM HALSTEAD 42 [John 38] b 1818.

WILLIAM J 43 [John 19] of New Windsor

WILLIAM W 44 [Enos 1] of Fishkill

WILLIAM WOODWORTH 45 [Ebenezer 3] b 1825.

WILTSEY A 1 [Abraham 7]

WINIFRED 1 m (License) 6 Apr 1763 **Jotham Post.** [WRIGHT MARR, 60]

Winifred/Wyntie (Simonds/Symonds) wf [Jonathan 2]

WISE 1 enlisted 10 Apr 1758 in a Suffolk Co NY Militia. [NY Muster Rolls in NYHS Vol 24]

WISE 2 [George 4] b Saybrook CT 13 Nov 1771 d Feb 1845 m 1792 **Abigail Soule.** Res Durham, Greene Co NY. Issue: Sarah 1794, Olive 1798, Wise Jr 1800, Fanny 1802, Matilda 1807, Harriet 1809, Eber, William Bradford 1813, Angeline 1815/16. Source adds (but doubtful) Philander 1831, Orrin 1833, Phebe Ann 1838, Henrietta 1837, Edgar Wise 1840, Lucinda 1842. [ONE LINE by Cone]

WOOLSEY 1 [Enos 1]

X Y Z

YMAR 1 [Isaac 3]

ZADOCK 1 [Anthony 4]

ZEBULON 1 [Gideon 2] b Oyster Bay LI 23 May 1710 d prob 13 Nov 1746 bur Underhill-Feke Cem, Matinicock LI perh m ca 1734 **Clement Feake** b Oyster Bay LI dau Rev Robert & Clemence (Ludlam) Feake. Blacksmith. Will 9 Nov 1746 proved 6 Dec 1746 names wf Clemence, son Daniel, unborn ch, bro Elijah. Exec bro/law Charles Feake. Issue: Daniel, prob Margaret m 1) Noah Townsend 2) Daniel Thorne 3) John Jackson. [NYCoNY PR 16:60 in NYHS 28:165; "The Feake Family Family of Norfolk, London, and Colonial America," by George E McCracken, in RECORD (1956), 87:109; "Early History of the Thorne Family," by Thorn Dickinson, in RECORD (1964), 95:149]

ZEBULON 2 [John 6] b perh Huntington LI 16 Apr 1747. Taxed Fredericksburgh Pct 1777. In DutCoNY Court (with Wm Wright) 1779, ordered to "keep peace with Daniel Ketcham". [WRIGHT RECORDS by Stark; PUTNAM COUNTY by Pelletreau, 127; DutCoNY Ancient Rec #9909]

ZEBULON 3 [Elijah 1]

ZEBULON 4 [William 2] b 1776.

ZERVIAH 1 [Edmund 2] b by 1731 m **John Wright**. See JOHN 15.

Zilla (Anderson) wf [Lewis 1]
Zilla (Hart) wf [James 17]

ZILPHA 1 [Gilbert 5] b 1832.

Zilpha (Baldwin) wf [Solomon 3]

ZIPPORAH/ZEBORAH 1 [? Anthony 2] m Richmond NY 14 Jan 1747 **John Androvit.** [WRIGHT MARR, 60]

Zipporah (Coles) wf [William 6]

ANNOTATED BIBLIOGRAPHY

ABEL WRIGHT by Stephen Wright
Wright, Rev. Stephen. "Descendants of Abel Wright of Springfield, Mass.", *NEHG Register* (1881).

ALBANY CO HIST
Parker, Amasa J. *Landmarks of Albany County, New York* (1897).

ALBANY WILLS
Fernow, Berthold (ed). *Calendar of Wills on File and Recorded in the Office of the Clerk of the Court of Appeals of the County Clerk at Albany, 1626-1836.* Society of Colonial Dames (1896).

BARTON GEN
McCracken, George E. "Roger Barton of Westchester County, N.Y.", *NEHG Register*, Vol 107.

Beaver Dam RDC Rec
"Records of the Reformed Dutch Church of Beaver Dam in the Town of Berne". Bound MSS in the NY State Library, Albany NY.

BERNE BURIALS
"Burying Ground Inscriptions, Town of Berne." *Yearbook of Dutch Settlers of Albany*, Vol 21 (1945-47), pp 26-87. NY State Library, Albany NY.

BETHLEHEM RECORDS by Christof
Christoph, Florence, and Christoph, Peter R. *Records of the People of the Town of Bethlehem, 1698-1880.* 1982.

COLE GEN
Cole, Frank T. *Early Genealogies of the Cole Families in America*. Columbus OH, 1887.

CORNELIUS LEDGER
Lamers, Claire M. (ed) "The Ledger of Doctor Elias Cornelius (1781-1810)", in *NYG&B Record* (1981), Vol. 112. Payment records of the physician of Phillipstown, Frederickstown, Carmel, Yorktown, and Somers.

Coxsackie RDC Rec
"Baptisms of the Dutch Reformed Church of Coxsackie, Greene County, New York" in the *NYG&B Record* (1960), Vol. 91.

CRUM ELBOW TAX LISTS
Buck, Clifford M. *Tax Lists, Crum Elbow, Nine Partners*. Salt Point NY. Includes Nine Partners Precinct 1738/39, Crum Elbow Precinct (1739/40 to Feb. 1762), Charlotte Precinct (June 1762 to 1779), Amenia Precinct (June 1762 to 1778), Clinton Precinct (probably 1786), Washington Precinct (probably 1786).

DUANESBURG QUAKER REC
"Duanesburg Quaker Records", *Utah Genealogical and Historical Magazine*, 4:48.

DUTCHESS COUNTY HIST
Commemorative Biographical Record of Dutchess County, New York (1897).

Elmhurst Presby Ch Rec
"Records of the Presbyterian Church (now Elmhurst), Queens County, Long Island, New York", *NYG&B Record* (1925), Vol. 56.

Fishkill RDC Rec
"Marriages of the Dutch Reformed Church, Fishkill, Dutchess County, New York," in the *NYG&B Record* (1952), Vol. 83. Baptisms 1731-1820, Marriages 1831-1820. Also in NY DAR Cemetery Collection 54:5ff.

FISHKILL TOMBSTONES
Van Vooris, E.W., compiler. *Tombstone Inscriptions from the Churchyard of the First Reformed Dutch Church of Fishkill Village, Dutchess Co., N.Y.* (1882). Privately printed.

400 YEARS by Larry Wright
Wright, Larry C. *Wright's 400 Years-Plus.* Amarillo TX: Whitney/Russell Printers, 1984. Good expecially for early New Jersey Wrights.

GRACE CH by Ladd
Ladd, H.O. *Origin and History of Grace Church of Jamaica, New York* (1914).

HAIGHT GEN by Hoyt
Hoyt, David W. *A Genealogical History of the Hoyt, Haight, and Hight Families.* (1984).

HANNAY PAPERS
Records of Major Hannay, in the Albany Historical and Literary Institution Library, Albany NY.

HUDSON-MOHAWK VALLEY
Reynolds, Cuyler. *Genealogical and Family Memoirs of Hudson-Mohawk Valley.*

LATTING FAM
Latting, John J. "The Latting Family," *NYG&B Record* (1871), Vol 2.

LOYALIST LINEAGES
Toronto Branch United Empire Loyalists Association of Canada (ed). *Loyalist Lineages of Canada, 1783-1983.* Toronto: Generation Press, 1984.

NEWTOWN MINUTES
Town Minutes of Newtown [NY] 1653-1734. Historical Records Survey, New York. 2 Volumes. 1941.

NINE PARTNERS by Buck
Buck, Clifford M. *Eighteenth Century Documents of Nine Partners Patent*. 1979.

NY MARR
Names of Persons for Whom Marriage Licenses were issued by the Secretary of the Province of New York to 1784. 1860.

NY PENSION ROLL
New York Pension Roll. Report from the Secretary of War (1935).

NY Presby Ch Rec
"Marriages in the 1st and Second Presbyterian Church, New York City," in *NYG&B Record*, Vol 4ff.

NYHS
New York Muster Rolls, 1755-1764. NY Historical Society Collection, Vol 24 (1891).

Early Wills, prior to 1800. NY Historical Society Collection, Vols 25-39 (1892-1908). Use with care, and, where possible, consult original documents.

ONE LINE by Cone
Cone, Mary Isabel Gibson. "One Line of the Wright Family". (n.d) but after 1940). Descendants of George Wright Sr of Durham, Greene Co NY, son of James Wright of Saybrook CT.

Port Richmond RDC Rec
"Records of the Reformed Dutch Church, Port Richmond, Staten Island, N.Y.," in *NYG&B Record* (1905-6), Vols 37-37.

Poughkeepsie Christ Ch Rec
Records of Christ Church, Poughkeepsie, 1777-1916.

POUGHKEEPSIE CEM by Frost
Frost, Josephine C. *Cemetery Inscriptions from Poughkeepsie, N.Y.* (1911). Bound MSS in NY State Library, Albany NY.

POUGHKEEPSIE M&D by Reynolds
Reynolds, Helen W. (ed) *Marriages and Deaths from Poughkeepsie NY Newspapers 1788-1825.* Dutchess County Historical Society, Vol. 4. (1930).

Poughkeepsie RDC Rec
First Dutch Reformed Church, Poughkeepsie, 1716-1913.

PUTNAM COUNTY HIST by Pelletreau
Pelletreau. *History of Putnam County, New York* (1886).

Rensselaerville Rec
"Rensselaerville Records, 1839-1903". Records of the former 1st Methodist Church of Rensselaerville NY. MSS in NY State Library, Albany NY.

Rhinebeck RDC Rec
Kelly, Arthur M. *Marriage Records of the Four Reformed Congregations of Old Rhinebeck, 1731-1899.* 1971.

SCHOHARIE CO OBITS
"Schoharie County, N.Y., Obituaries, from the File of the Schoharie Republican." Card file in the NY State Library, Albany NY.

SCJ
Roebling, Emily Warren. *The Journal of The Rev. Silas Constant.* (1903).

THORNE FAM
Dickinson, Thorn. "Early History of the Thorne Family," *NYG&B Record* (1964), Vol. 95.

UNDERHILL GEN
Frost, Josephine C. *Underhill Genealogy*, Vol 2 (1932)

Watervliet RDC Rec
"Marriages in the Reformed Dutch Church, Watervliet, 1784-1850", in *Tree Talks*, Albany County, pp 1-3.

WESTCHESTER COUNTY HIST by Bolton
Bolton, Robert. *History of the County of Westchester*. 2 Volumes (1848).

WESTCHESTER COUNTY HIST by Scharf
Scharf. *History of Westchester County, New York*. 1886.

WILTSIE FAM by Zabriske
Zabriske, George Olin. "The Wiltsie Family of Early New York," *NYG&B Record* (1976), Volume 107.

WRIGHT BOOK by Maerz
Maerz, Claudette. *Wright Book of Family Ancestry Sheets*. Vol. 1. Bloomington IN [nd]. Compiled ancestry sheets from correspondents. NEHGS, Boston.

WRIGHT FAMILY by Henry W. Wright
Wright, Rev. Henry W. *Genealogy of the Wright Family from 1639 to 1901*. Middletown CT: Pelton & King, 1901. Descendants of Benjamin Wright of Guilford CT.

WRIGHT FAMILY RECORD by Joe Wright
"Wright Family Record," contributed by Joseph V. Wright, in *National Genealogical Society Quarterly*, 61:145. Bible record of Samuel Wright of Clinton, cordwainer, and his son-in-law Joseph Wright of Berne NY.

WRIGHT MARR
"Wright Marriages in New York," in *Genealogy* (April 1917), 7:49-60.

WRIGHT/FL by Perrine
Perrine, Howland Delano. "Jonathan Wright of Flushing, L.I., 1509-192-". South Orange NJ. MSS, in NYG&BS Library, New York NY.

WRIGHT/OB by Latting
Latting, John J. "The Wright Family of Oyster Bay, L.I.", *NYG&B Record* (1872), 3:35-45.

WRIGHT/OB by Perrine
Perrine, Howland Delano. *The Wright Family of Oyster Bay, L.I.* (1923). Standard work on a large Long Island family.

WRIGHT RECORDS by Stark
Stark, Helen. "Wright Family Records," in *The American Genealogist*, 14:160-162. Account Book of Gideon Wright, of Oyster Bay, Long Island, begun in 1702.

WRIGHTS OF LONG ISLAND by Francis Wright
Wright, Francis and Cleghorn, Maude E. (White). "Wright of Long Island". MSS of one line of descent from David Wright, son of Jonathan Wright of Flushing, L.I.

APPENDIX

WRIGHT ESTATES FILED AFTER 1800

Greene County Surrogate Court, Catskill NY

Wills:

Name	Docket	Liber	Year	Town
George	480-10587	(B:92)		
Joseph	480-10618	(C:446)		Durham
Abel	480-10639	(D:166)	1837	Coxsackie
Joseph	480-10618	(C:446)	1835	
William	480-10640	(D:166)	1840	Coxsackie
Peter D	482-10700	(G:440)		Coxsackie
Ambrose	482-10724			
Elizabeth	484-10760	(I:383)		
Temperance	484-10792	(J:273)		Durham
Olney F	485-10794	(J:386)	1864	Coxsackie
Sarah	487-10838	(M:84)	1877	
Oliver	493-10982	(O:213)	1891	Durham
Harriet M	495-11020	(Q:151)	1891	

Administrations:

Name	Docket	Liber
James	481-10647	(D:77)
Benjamin	482-10685	(F:54)
Oscar F	482-10704	(G:54)
Christopher	483-10733	(H:79)
Horatio N	484-10748	(H:317)
Silas	488-10879	(J:346)
Margaret	492-10945	(K:82)
John F	492-10945	(K:83)
William	492-10949	(K:128)

Guardianships:

George	480-10604	(E:149)
Peter D	480-10629	(C:68)
John H	480-10630	(C:70)
Helen L	481-10648	(D:20)
James H	481-10649	(D:26)

Columbia County Surrogate Court, Hudson NY

Name	Liber	Year
Wills:		
Rachel	(G:350)	1835
Thomas	(J:629)	1844
George	(L:226)	1858
Belden	(M:725)	1864
Horatio N	(N:447)	1866

Dutchess County Surrogate Court, Po'keepsie NY

Name	Docket	Liber	Year	Place
Wills:				
Charles C	1710X		1842	Northeast
Abraham D	1891		1848	Pl Valley
Elizabeth	2040		1849	
Isaac R	2323		1851	Virginia
Sylvia	2276		1853	Unionvale
Solon	2379		1854	
Anderson	3125		1867	Lagrange
Amelia	3439	(J:155)	1835	Po'k
Elijah	3519	(J:485)	1837	Pl Valley
Abraham B	3707	(M:313)	1841	Lodi NJ
Isaac	3778	(M:439)	1842	Fishkill
Joseph	3999	(O:498)	1846	Milan
Enos	4615	(S:437)	1855	Fishkill
Robert	4743	(S:604)	1855	E Fishkill
Eliza	5697	(W:434)	1867	Fishkill
Jonathan	6579	(Z:585)	1871	E Fishkill

```
Wiltsie A    6063                  1857  Louisiana
William M    8600                  1876  E Fishkill
William      10274    (8:16)       1882  Beekman
William H    12440    (9:622)      1888
```

Administrations:

```
John       177
Joseph     223
Ebenezer   438                     1806  Carmel
Isaac      438                           Carmel
```

Albany County Surrogate Court, Albany NY

Name	Liber	Year
Wills:		
Samuel	(8:82)	1832
John	(12:266)	1844
Nathaniel	(17:167)	1860
George	(22:418)	1871
Charles C	(24:208)	1874
Clarissa	(24:373)	1874
Administrations:		
John	(5:15)	1824
Maria	(5:32)	1825
John	(5:103)	1827
Samuel	(7b:299)	1847
Thomas	(7b:301)	1847
Jacob	(11:72)	1866
James J	(12:219)	1872

Orange County Surrogate Court, Goshen NY

Name	Liber	Year	Place
Wills:			
David	(J:351)	1835	Newburgh
John	(K:231)	1838	New Windsor

Matilda	(S:270)	1852	Warwick
Susan	(T:237)	1852	Newburgh
Augustus	(U:163)	1854	Newburgh

Administrations:

Benjamin	(E:116)	1819	Newburgh
Anannias	(F:32)	1829	Warwick
Mary Elizabeth	(I:236)	1857	Bloomingv
John	(J:10)	1858	Cornwall

Letters Testamentary:

John	(A:46)		New Windsor
Matilda	(C:94)	1852	Warwick
Susan	(C:171)	1854	Newburgh

PLACE INDEX

NEW YORK

Addison
  13
Albany
  13,24,73,75,91,99,
  125
Albany County
  16,29,98,131,136
Amawalk
  119,120
Amenia
  16,124
Argyle
  64,65
Bangall
  64
Barbourville
  3
Barre
  95
Bedford
  12,37,64
Beekman
  22,45,46,53,65,71,
  72,82,83,112,117,
  153
Berne
  3,13,26,28,32,38,
  58,62,73,76,80,82,
  83,84,87,95,108,
  109,113,119,125,
  127,135,137,138

Bethlehem
  2,88,99,137
Bloomingvale
  154
Brinkerhoffville
  51
Brooklyn
  77
Broome
  48
Cambridge
  15
Carlisle
  24
Carmel
  15,29,31,48,65,77,
  114,125,126,130,153
Cedar Swamp
  81
Chatham
  22
Charlotte Pct
  62,125
Clinton
  7,23,38,62,74,85,
  108,125
Cobelskill
  62,131
Coeymans
  38,85,137
Cold Spring
  46,58,65

Cooperstown
  76,77,97
Cornwall
  154
Cortlandt Manor
  2,69
Cortlandt
  61,65,69,83,111
Coxsackie
  1,110,120,130,137,
  151
Croton Falls
  48,114
Crum Elbow
  21,22,61,121
Delaware County
  35
Delhi
  24
Durham
  46,83,112,139,151
Dutchess County
  35,63,84,108,113,
  118,122,124,130,
  136,137,141
Duanesburg
  29,75,85
Eastchester
  34,75,78,125,129,
  135
Esperance
  16,76,113
Fishkill
(Also E Fishkill)
  3,17,23,28,33,34,
  35,37,45,46,48,49,
  51,53,57,58,61,62,
  65,66,68,71,72,75,
  79,82,83,84,89,100,
  112,115,117,121,
  123,125,130,131,
  133,136,138,152,153
Florida
  75

Flushing
  7,6,21,24,25,41,45,
  51,52,53,63,67,70,
  71,78,79,80,91,94,
  113,115,117,120,
  133,135,137
Franklin
  64,80
Fredericksburgh Pct
  27,63,79,114,115,
  133,141
Frederickstown
  2,29,31,37,38,89,
  114
Freehold
  46,82
Freeman
  85
Gallopsville
  8,136
Goshen
  130
Gravesend
  45
Greene County
  82
Halfmoon
  138
Hempstead
  25,41,42,57,68,73,
  77,83,88,107,118,
  120,136
Highland Falls
  97
Hopewell
  23,35,76,130
Hopkinton
  7
Huntington
  6,9,11,51,71,84,
  133,141
Hunt's Point
  52,97

Jamaica
  11,17,63,68,88,94,
  126
Jericho
  12,81,125
Kent
  28,31,37,72,76
Kinderhook
  22
Kingsbury
  3
LaGrange
  58,88,130,152
Lewisboro
  17
Linlithgo
  38
Little Nine Partners
  64
Mahopac
  136
Maryland
  22
Middleburg
  66,76
Milan
  57,82
Mill Neck
  127
Mt Pleasant
  74,100
New Hackensack
  23,122
New Hamburgh
  48
New Purchase
  64
New Rochelle
  74
New Windsor
  12,25,28,34,69,73,
  75,77,102,153,154
New York City
  5,24,64,72,73,74,
  81,82,83,85,125,
  129,136
Newburgh
  25,77,83,121,153,
  154
Newcastle
  15,64,94,122,137
Newtown
  17,26,45,49,68,78,
  79,81,92,117
Nine Partners
  7,22,62,64,69,74,
  81,124,125,135
North Castle
  17,42,65,73,113,
  122,131,134
North Hempstead
  125
Northeast
  18,42,62,64,152
Norwich
  4,31
Onondaga County
  4,137
Ontario County
  118
Orange County
  130
Otsego County
  75
Ovid
  136
Oxford
  58
Oyster Bay
  1,4,8,9,12,15,23,
  27,30,31,32,33,47,
  48,64,68,69,71,72,
  84,87,91,94,103,
  107,108,111,113,
  115,129,133,135,141
Patterson
  27,46

Peekskill
  25,32,67,74,121,124
Pelham Manor
  135
Philipse Pct
  80,138
Philipstown
  17,35,37,41,46,82,
  127,130,131,133,137
Pine Plains
  32
Pleasant Valley
  3,31,42,95,123,133,
  152
Port Richmond
  53,61,131,142
Poughkeepsie
  3,22,45,54,62,66,
  77,83,93,115,121,
  126,137,152
Putnam County
  134
Queens County
  68,71,79,125,133
Rhinebeck
  73,80,83,109
Richmond
  7
Richmondville
  24,27,133
Rochester
  1
Rome
  118,131
Rumbout
  21,67,74,81,83,88,
  111,136
Rye
  51,84,93
Salem
  118
Saratoga Patent
  69
Schenectady
  76,119
Schoharie
  26,113
Schoharie County
  32,63
Shappagua
  122
Smithtown
  21,47,48
Smithville Flats
  22
Somers
  12,23,32,57,61,69,
  77,92,97,98,100,
  102,110,112,121
Somers Plains
  17
Southeast
  30,126
South Hempstead
  102
Stanford
  57,82
Staten Island
  8,53,54,77,129
Stephentown AlbCo
  135
Stephentown WestCo
  2,11,12,23,35,61,
  98,111,112,113,121
Steuben County
  24
Stockport
  112
Stormville
  3,24,46
Suckscally Wigwam
  72
Suffolk County
  125,139
Syracuse
  137
Terrytown
  84

Troy
 112
Ulster County
 25,72
Union
 82,4
Union Valley
 23
Unionvale
 152
Utica
 118
Warwick
 25,136,154
Washington
 64
Westbury
 18,41,69,81
Westerlo
 29,77
Westchester County
 34,63,65,71,92,93,
 94,95,98,114,124,
 125,126,127,130,
 134
Westford
 75
Westport
 22
Wheatley
 80
Whitestown
 45,118
White Plains
 67,94
Wright
 26
Wrightstreet
 46
Yorktown
 3,11,12,21,38,41,
 70,98,110,124

ALABAMA

Oswichee
 65

CONNECTICUT

Chatham
 97
Danbury
 35
Hebron
 22,93
Horseneck
 64
Lebanon
 37,71
Mansfield
 2
Middletown
 22,29
Ridgefield
 92
Saybrook
 5,46,139
Stamford
 71
Sharon
 18
Westport
 27,105
Windham
 93

ILLINOIS

Elgin
 125

INDIANA

Dearborn County
 108
Caesar 118

KENTUCKY

Bourbon County
108

LOUISIANA

New Orleans
65
State of
153

MARYLAND

Worcester County
9

MASSACHUSETTS

Braintree
45
Lynn
69,103
Rehoboth
45,78
Salem
45
Sandwich
103

MICHIGAN State of
1

MISSISSIPPI

Pass Christian
65
Vicksburg
66

NEW JERSEY

Burlington
61

Lebanon
98
Lodi
152
Ridgefield
2,92
Trenton
61
Woodbridge
79

OHIO

Blendon
19
Cleveland
13
New Garden
85

PENNSYLVANIA

Whiteland
61

RHODE ISLAND

Newport
107
North Kingstown
107

VERMONT

Bennington
107
Monkton
1
Rutland
124
Shaftsbury
107

Weybridge
  16

VIRGINIA

Botetourt County
  108
Cowpasture River
  131
Fairfax
  58,63,115
Jackson's River
  108
State of
  107,152

WISCONSIN

Orfordville
  58
Rock Counry
  4
State of
  13

CANADA

Bedeque PEI
  102
Canada West
  122
Lower Bedeque PEI
  126
St John's NB
  127
Tryon PEI
  102,126

ENGLAND

Cronton
  70
Liverpool
  70
London
  77
Norfolk County
  102

HOLLAND 118

IRELAND 72

SCOTLAND

Ettrick Forest
  133

NAME INDEX

ADAMS
  Nathan 105
  Sarah 105
ADRIANCE
  Theodore 83
ALLEN
  Jane 3
  Jasper 33
  Joseph 3
  Judah 82
ALSOP
  Amy wf 79
  Hannah (---) 79
  Richard 79
ANDREWS
  Mary 8
  Samuel 107
ANTHONY
  William 38
AORSON
  Aaron 119
ATCHISON
  Hugh 64
AUSTIN
  Almerin 112
  Louisa 112
BABCOCK
  Sarah 3
  Simon 112
BAILEY
  Amos 137
  Edward 70
  Elizabeth 64
  John (Rev) 97

  John 57
  Ruth wf JOHN 6
BAKER
  Amelia 57
  Elizabeth 107
BANKER
  Elizabeth 130
BALDWIN
  Elisha 125
  Elizabeth (Cromwell) 125
  Zilpha 125
  Zippora 80
BARKER
  Abigail 71
  Naomy 113
BARLOW
  Walter 46
BARTON
  Caleb 88, 124
  Elizabeth 124
  Gabriel 88, 119, 124
  Mary 73
  William 88
BARTOW/BARTOE
  Anthony 75
  Charity 75
  Cornelius Stevenson 75
  Mary Annah 80
  Phebe 75
BARNES
  Daniel 52
BARTLETT
  Edmund 46

BASSETT
  Susan 75
BAVELOT
  John 70
BAYLEY
  Harvey Newell 15
BAXTER
  ---- 51
  Elisha C 41
BEAUMONT
  --- 95, 135
BEAUPRE
  Ann 101
BEADLE/BEDELL
  David 12, 98
  Ephraim 12, 98
  Elizabeth 12
  Philena (Frost)
    12, 98
BENNET
  Margaret 68
  Mariah (Duryea) 68
  Nicholas 68
BENTLEY
  --- 136
BETTS
  William 78
BEYEA/BOUYEA
  I. 117
BILL
  Patience 22
BIRCH
  Jeremiah 81, 94
BIRCK
  George Wallace 41, 135
BIRDSALL
  Samuel 30, 120
BLAIN
  Jane 136
BLAKE
  Catherine 131
BLIVEN
  Charles 38
BLOOMER
  Beverly 41

BLOOM/BLOOMS
  Margaret 108
  Rebecca 118
BLOOMFIELD
  Ezekiel 79
  Hannah 79
BOARDMAN
  Theodore 135
BONDET
  --- 8
BOUCK
  Sarah 76
BRADY
  Mary 74
BRIEN
  John 94
BRIGGS
  Susan 29
BRINKERHOFF
  Dirck 81
  Derick 22
  Susan H 3
BROOK/BROOKS
  John 47
  Jonathan 79
BROWN
  Andrew 80
  Phebe 26
  William 3
BRUNDIGE
  Andrew 114
BURNETT
  David 109
BURR
  John 68, 87
BURRELL
  Sarah 138
BURT
  Phebe 3
BUSH
  Marritje 75
  Zachariah 75
BUTLER
  Zebulon 51

BUYS
  Abraham 45
  Rebecca 45
CAMRON
  Eavon 42
CANDEE
  Isaac 98, 111
CANFIELD
  Phineas 46
CARMAN
  John 28
  Samuel 11, 121
CARPENTER
  Daniel 121
  Elizabeth 72
  Ephraim 72
  Hannah (Canfield) 72
  Samuel 68
  Ursula 68
CARHART
  John 98
CATHCART
  John 23
CHAMPENOIS
  Daniel 80
CHAPIN
  Tirza 16
CHASE/CHACE
  Rebecca 133
CHEESMAN
  Joseph 119
  Phebe 119
  Ruth 74
CLARK/CLARKE
  Cynthia 65
  William H 1
COBBIT
  Lydia 129
COCK
  Daniel 48
  George 48
  Levi 23
COLE/COLES/COALS
  Charity (Valentine) 135
  Eber 46
  Freelove 15
  Joseph 15, 33, 135
  Nathaniel 92, 70, 101, 115
  Robert 98, 101
  Wright 15
  Zipporah 135
COLWELL
  Charles 35
  Hetty 58
  Polly (Smith) 58
  Samuel 18, 57, 58
  Sarah 137
CONKLIN
  Jacob 64
COOKES
  Robert 7, 72
COOPER
  Elizabeth A 129
  Joseph 101, 121, 129
  Mary (Wright) 15
CORNELIUS
  Dr Elias 64, 65, 72, 98, 113, 117, 134
CRABBE
  Alice (---) 8
  Richard 107
  Richard 8
CRAFT
  Elijah 136
CRANE
  Elizabeth 130
  Martha (Townsend) 130
  Nathaniel 130
CROWL
  Roxana 24
CUNNINGHAM
  Abbie 24
  Mary Ann 15
  Marian 15, 114
  Marian (Mosher) 15, 114
  Shubel 15, 114
CURRY
  Joseph 114
  Richard 114

CURTISS
  Clarissa 29
DAVENPORT
  John 46
  Lewis 118
  Martha 118
  Martha (---) 118
  Mary (Snook) 46
  Mary Susan 46
DAY
  Ann 81
  Hannah 81
  John 81
DEAN
  David 134
  Smith Austin 27, 114
DEARING
  John 48, 66
DELAVAN
  Mary (Thompson) 121
DENIKE
  Samuel 67
DENNIS
  Mary 4
DEMPSEY
  Margaret 109
DENTON
  Clarissa (Fowler) 65
  Martha 65
  Solomon 65
DICKINSON
  Elizabeth 15
  James 30
  Mary 47
DICKSON
  Thomas 93
DINGY
  Robert 81
DOANE
  Daniel 122
DODGE
  Martha 125
DOGED
  John 78
DRAKE

Moses 52, 79
Richard 79
Stephen 79
DUNBAR
  Collin 112
  Elizabeth 112
  George 112
  Harriet Jane 112
  Mary 112
  William 112
DUNWOODY
  --- s/l 137
DURLAND/DORLAND
  Ann 31
  John 31
  Mary (Birdsall) 31
DUSENBURY
  Elizabeth 84, 85
EATON
  Mary (Wood) 26
ECKERSON
  Annatye 76
ELLIOTT
  Jacob 22
ELLIS
  Esther 112
ELLISON
  Thomas 68
EVERETT
  Abraham 120
  William 82
FARRINGTON
  Benjamin 4, 27
FEAKE/FEKE
  Charles 141
  Clemence (Ludlam) 141
  Clement 141
  John 1, 71
  Robert 141
FERGUSON
  Eleazer 35, 114
FIELD
  --- 21
  Abijah 111
  Hazard 21, 41

FIELD cont.
  John 41, 70
  Lydia 41
FISH
  --- 94
  Elizabeth 94
FISK
  Elizabeth 112
  Henry 112
  Polly 112
  William 112
FLOYD
  Margaret 74
FORD
  Thomas 53
FORDHAM
  Martha 12
FORMAN
  Jacob 12
  Jemima (Ryder) 12
  Mary A 12
FOWLER
  Duncan 41
  Jacob 78
  Joseph 124
  Martha 41
  Mary 124
  Sarah (Whitney) 124
FOX
  Catherine 118
FRANKLIN
  Henry 68
  Walter 48
FROST
  Anne 121
  Caroline 76
  Daniel Wright 121
  Elizabeth 121
  Ethelannah 80
  Ezra f/l 76
  Hannah 87
  Jacob 21, 111, 120
  James 76
  Joel 11
  John 4, 111

  Keziah (Wright) 120
  Mary (March) 76
  Mary (Wallace) 76
  Rachel 121
  Rebecca (Wright) 8
  Samuel 87, 120
  Sally Ann 76
  William 87, 101
FULLER
  Martha 37
FURMAN
  Elizabeth 94
  Jonathan 94
  Josiah 93
  Samuel 94
GAMONG
  Abel 114
GANSEVOORT
  Peter 119
GARDNER/GARDINER
  --- 62
  Daniel 26
  Mercy (Burtch) 26
  Phebe 26
GLEANEE
  Anthony 53
GOODRICH
  Abigail 19
  Abigail (---) 19
  Bela 19
GOODSELL
  Herman 35
GREEN/GREENE
  Lois 3
  Nancy 29
  Naomi (Cummins) 3
  Robert 3
GREGG
  Jane 12
GRIFFIN
  Jacob 16, 78
  John 113
  Mary 63
GRISWOLD
  Thomas 131

GROSBECK
  Anna (Bajeau) 129
  Johannes 129
GUERNSEY
  Clark 57
HAIGHT
  Bathsheba (---) 122
  Beverly 51
  Daniel 51, 135
  Elizabeth 61
  Esther 51
  Hannah 51
  James 122
  Jemima 135
  John 51
  Joseph 51, 70
  Mary 51
  Phebe 51
  Reuben 113, 122
  Samuel 111, 114
  Sylvanus 51
  William 51
HALL
  Sarah 65
HALLETT
  Bridgett 81
  John 11, 17
  Samuel 81, 121
HALLOCK
  Jesse 34, 113
HALSEY
  Meliscent 5
HALSTEAD
  Charles 121
  David 25
  Gershom 75, 82, 121
  Mary (Smith) 75
  Mary 82
  Phebe 75, 82
HAMILTON
  Mary 57
  Mercer 57
HAMMOND
  Betsey 64
  Joshua 7, 72

HANES
  George 18
  Meria (---) 18
HARRISON
  Isaiah 47
HART
  Hannah 83
  Hannah (Garrison) 65
  Samuel 65
  Zilla 65
HARRIS/HARICE
  Benjamin 64
HARVEY
  George 94
HAVILAND
  Daniel Wright 109
  Ebenezer 109
  Esther 109
  Gilbert 21, 109
  Sarah 109
HAWXHURST/HAWKHURST
  Jerusha (Smith) 125
  Mary 125
  Samson 125
  Susannah 27
  Thomas 64, 122
HAYES
  John 95
  Maria 95
  Mary 95
  Nancy 95
  Thomas 34, 95, 119
HAZARD
  Amy (Alsop) 79
  Nathaniel 79
HEMPSTEAD
  Joseph 116
HENRY
  Ann 81
  Margaret 135
HICKS
  Charity (Wright) 18
  Lawrence 18
HILDRETH
  Benjamin 131

HOLDEN
  Daniel 136
HORNER
  Isaac 107
HORTON
  --- 25, 135
  Daniel 21, 94, 124
  David 93
  Elizabeth (Lee) 67, 121
  Esther 124
  Esther (Lane) 21, 94, 124
  Esther (King) 93
  John 67, 121
  Joseph 21
  Mary 93
  Mercy Ann 57
  Nathan 42
  Rachel 21
  Richard 67
  Stephen 94
  Thomas 93
  William 112, 118, 121
HOTCHKISS
  Addison 112
  Ann Amelia 112
  Eliza 112
  Henry 112
  Jeremiah 112
  Rachel 112
  Samuel E 112
HOWE
  Janet 57
HOWELL
  Thomas 94
HOWMAN
  James 64
HUTCHINS
  Lucretia 108
HUBBARD
  --- 91, 23
HUGHART
  Agnes (Jordon) 108
  Jane 108
  James 108

HULL
  Moses 101, 118
  Sarah 65
HUNT
  --- 2, 11, 34
  James 75
  Jonathan 117
  Thomas 52, 79, 97
HUYCK
  Sarah 130
JACKSON
  John 91
  Obadiah 48
  Phebe 48
JAMES
  Benjamin 11
JEACOCKS
  Mary 23
JONES
  John J 67, 135
KEELER
  --- 25
KELLEY
  Roger 22
KETCHAM
  Daniel 141
KIPP
  Magdelen 68
KIRK
  Arthur 4
  Benjamin 81
  Elizabeth 4
  Temperance 81
  Temperance (Seaman) 4
KNAPP
  Allen 38
  Enoch 21, 38
  James 38
  Joseph 98
  Milicent 98
  Prudence 38
KRONK
  Delilah 76
KNOWELS
  Martha 118

LAMONT
  Archibald 63
LANE
  Robert 61
LANGDON
  Ananias 67
LANGFORD
  Betsey 85
LASHLY
  Mary 82
LATHAM
  Joseph 84
LATTIN/LATTING
  Adolphus 1
  Benjamin 1, 42
  Deborah 42
  Deborah (Holmes) 1
  Elijah Belden 95
  Freelove 42
  Joseph 93, 95
  Josiah 101, 120
  Leah (Simonson) 42
  Nathaniel 95
  Sally (---) 95
  Sarah 42
  Sarah (Wright) 8
  Wright 42
LAWRENCE
  Rachel 74
LAY
  Anna 46
LEAK
  Emeline 83
LEE
  --- 57, 70, 115, 117, 120
  Charles (Gen.) 63
  Elizabeth (Curry) 114
  Elizabeth 63
  Ruth 57
LEVERICH
  Caleb 68
  Eleazer 101
  Mary 68
  Samuel 26

LEWIS
  Esther 97
  Jordon 41
LIMMER
  Peter 136
LOCKWOOD
  Jonathan 42, 71
LONDON
  Susan 118
LOOMIS
  Samuel 19
LORD
  Ann 102
  Frances 126
LOUDON
  Samuel 77
LOUNSBERRY
  Isaac 134
LUDLAM
  --- 18, 27
  Elizabeth (Townsend) 71
  Joseph 71
  Sarah 71
LYONS
  Sarah 134
MAGRA
  Sarah 92
MARLING/MARLYN
  Aaltje 53
MARSH
  Margaret 136
MAYBIE/MAYBEE
  Jeremiah 95
  John 114
Mc CLAUGHREY
  James 25
Mc FARLAND
  Sarah Jane 74
Mc INTOSH
  Elizabeth 99
  Stephen 99
  William 9
Mc KEEL
  John 51

Mc KINLEY
  William 77
Mc QUIRREY
  Mary 130
Mc WHIRK
  George 19
MEAD/MEDE/MEED
  Augusta Louise 46
  Isaac 101, 135
  Sarah 82
  Zebulon 135
MEKELL
  Sarah 17
  Uriah 17
MERRICK
  Dorinda 126
  Eliza (---) 126
  Ezra 126
MILES
  Jonathan 65
  Mariel (Hathaway) 65
MILLER
  Abigail (Crampton) 98
  Abraham H 12
  Dan C 12
  Increase 98
  Ruth 98
MONTANYE
  Jane 73
  Rebecca (---) 73
  Thomas 73
MORREL
  Sarah (West) 117
MORRIS
  John 32
MOSHER
  Johanna 114
MOTT
  Amy 82
  Joseph 82
NELSON
  Elizabeth (---) 121
  John 121
  Justus 46
  Katherine 46

Mary 22
Mary (Odell) 46
Meriam (---) 22
Mephibosheth 22
Reuben 125
Thomas 61, 121
Van Buren 138
NICHOLS
  --- 13
  Samuel 31, 42
NIXON
  Jane 74
NOE
  Loris 94
NUTT
  John 16
OGDENS
  Jonathan 63, 71
OLIVER
  James 119
OSBORNE
  Joseph 2
OWEN
  Ambrose 13, 23
  Diantha 13
  Uraline 13
  Uri 13
PALMER
  Henry 94
  Susanna 17
PATTERSON
  Amy 64
  Elizabeth 5
PELL
  Catherine 61
PEMBERTON
  Peter 70
PERRY
  Nathaniel 57
PHELPS
  Catherine 137
  Elijah B 115
  Perry 19
  William R 137

PHILIPS
  Martha 88
  James 35
  James 98
PIESTER
  Frederick 82
PINCKNEY
  --- 62
PLADDO
  Sara 136
PLATT
  Sophia 54
POCK
  John 64
POST
  Elizabeth 46
  Jotham 5, 11, 139
POWAS
  Mary 138
POWELL
  Hannah 94
PRATT
  Lucy 37
PRESTON
  --- 73
PROCTOR
  Mary 127
PROUT
  Timothy 7
PURDY
  Jacobus (Capt.) 134
  Milicent 11
PURNELL
  Elizabeth 9
  Thomas 9
PURRINGTON
  Joseph R 46
PUTNEY
  Mary 119
QUIMBY
  Ephraim 113
  Phebe 113
RADNER/RATNER
  Godfrey 1, 2, 119
  Jacob 2

John 23
Peggy 2
RANDALL
  --- 8
RAYNER/RAYNOR
  Sylvanus 2
READ
  Sarah 30
READER
  Temperance 25
REDDING
  William 1
REILLY
  Terance 122
REMSEN
  George 134
REYNOLDS
  Austin 73
RHODES
  Diana (---) 135
  Elizabeth 135
  John 135
  Mary 9, 47
RICHARDSON
  Mary 61
RICKEW
  Jacob 33
ROCHELL
  Elizabeth
    (Grosbeck) 129
ROGERS
  John 125
ROE/ROL/RAL
  Antje/Anna 61
ROWE/ROE
  Catherine 80
  David 78
ROSSETER
  Robert 1
SACKETT
  Joseph 68
SAITLEY/SAWTELL/SAWTELES
  Henry 78, 92
  Sarah 78

SALTER
  Manasseh 16
SAMMIS
  Keziah 21
  Tabiatha 84
SAYRE
  Bethia (Cooper) 105
  Jane 105
  Nehemiah 105
SCOTT
  Christina 66
SEAMAN
  Benjamin 81
  Martha (Titus) 81
  Mary 102
  Phebe 75
  Walter 64
SEARING
  Coe 48
SEARS
  Benjamin 30
SELLERS
  Elizabeth 73
SHAY
  Margaret (Urquehart) 47
SHED
  Daniel 102, 108
  Electa 131
  Elizabeth 108
  Lucy (Nutting) 108
  Sarah 102
SILLIMAN
  Daniel 46
SIMONDS/SYMONDS
  Jesse 64
  Winifred/Wyntie 78
SIMPKINS
  --- 71
  --- 111
SKIDMORE
  Joseph 102
  Mary 102
  Thomas 66
  Walter 102

SKINNER
  Abel 93
  Ann 93
  Christina 38
  Christopher 38
  Durthany 93
  Elizabeth 79
  Ephraim 93
  Esther 38
  Francis 38
  Hannah 93
  John 38
  Martha 38, 93
  Reuben 38
  Robert 38
  Sarah 38
  Thomas 93
  William 38
  Wright 38, 79
SLAGHT/SLACK
  Barent 54, 84
  Bond 9
  Christian 54
SLEETH
  Abraham 33
SLOAT/SLOTE
  Budd 15
  Charles 23
  Margery/Margaret 136
  Mary 23
  Susan (---) 23
SMALLEY
  Nathan 115
SMITH
  Benjamin 11
  Charlotte 121
  Elizabeth 17
  Isaac 45, 64, 89
  John 29, 113
  Mary 11
  Obadiah 49
  Sarah 112
  Susannah (Stephens) 27
  Tabitha 121
  Thomas 82

SPARKS
  Jonas 94
SOMENDYCK
  Catherine 74
SOULE
  Abigail 139
SOUTHWICK
  Eliza 83
SPRINGSTEEN
  Gerry 43, 80
STAN--
  Eli 137
STARK
  John 22
STIMPSON
  William 46
STOKES
  Jonathan 46
  Thomas 68, 111
STRATTON
  --- 136
STREVEL
  Harvey 127
  Isaac 27
  Matthew 32, 127
STURTEVANT
  Elias 22
STYAT
  --- 71
SUTHERLAND
  Lovina 22
SUTTON
  Andrew Pell 102
SWAN
  Cyrus 18
SWARTHOUT
  Jacob 45, 53, 73
SWEET
  Ralph 82
TALERDAY
  Henry 45
Ten EYCK
  Hannah 38
TERBUSH
  Capt. 53

THOMAS
  Anna (Sands) 21
THOMPSON
  Robert 130
THORNE
  Daniel 91
  Daniel 141
THORNTON
  Catherine 119
THURSTON
  Anne 24
  Hannah 24
  Joseph 24
TITUS
  Constant 17
TODD
  P. 80
TOWNSEND
  Ann (Cole) 70
  Eliphant 23
  Elizabeth 47
  Elizabeth (Montgomerie)
    47
  Hannah 61
  Henry 32, 70
  George 134
  John 47, 68, 70, 91,
    101, 121
  Mary 70
  Noah 91
  Rachel 68
  Robert 68
  Sarah 30
  Susannah (Harcourt) 68
TRACY
  Tryphena 79
TRAVIS
  David 15
TURNER
  James 1
UNDERHILL
  Mary 23, 54
VALENTINE
  John 33

Van ALSTINE
  Abraham 29
Van NOSTRAND
  Aaron 80
Van VLEEK/VanVLACK
  Aaron 35
  George 35
  John 35
Van WYCK
  Alanson 35
  Cornelis 35
  Jane 35
  John 35
  Maria 35
VAIL
  Mary 101
VANCE
  David 25, 51
VANDERGRIFT
  Ann 61
VANDUERSON
  Huyla 72
Van WYCK
  Sarah 74
VERMILYEA/VERMIYA
  Edward 69, 114
  Elizabeth (Asten) 88
  John 88
  Maria 88
VINCENT
  Lydia 113
Von VORHUS
  --- 58
WAGGONER
  Adam 62
WALKER
  William 93
WALTERS
  Sarah 23
WARNER/WARING
  --- 71, 110
WARREN
  Ann (Hustis) 58
  Mary 3
  Phebe 58
  Samuel 58
WASHBURN
  --- 134
  Abraham 101
  Daniel 101
  Isaac 101
  Jacob Cheesman 101
  Philena Wright 101
  Phylena (Matthews) 101
WEEKS
  Edmund 33, 71
  Jacob 69
WEIDMAN
  John 38
WELLS
  Sarah 130
WELSH
  Hannah 118
WEST
  Samuel 82
WHEELER
  --- 33, 78
  Patience 80
WHITAKER
  --- 136
WHITE
  Lucy 66
  Simon 108
  Theodosius 110
WHITNEY
  Seth 34, 61
WHITTEMORE
  Abigail 38
WILCOX
  Sarah 4
WILLIAMS
  Heber 58
  Margaret 133
  Martha (Bennett) 58
  Sally 58
  William F 126
WILLES/WILLIS
  Fry 31
  Hannah 94

WILLES/WILLIS cont
  Samuel 81, 94
  Stephen 38
  William 94
WILTSEY/WILTSIE/WILSEY
  Abraham 109
  Cornelius 108
  Eleanor 109
  Hendrick/Henricus/Henry
    108, 109
  Henry Teunissen 108
  Hester (Van Vleck) 108
  Jacob 109
  John 109
  Lavinia/Wyntje 109
  Margaret 119
  Phebe 109
  Reuben 108
  William 109
WINANS
  Wynant 8, 54
WINSTANLY/WINSTANLEY
  Edward 70
  Eleanor 70
  Nelly 70
  William 70
WOOD
  Hannah 37
  George 78, 92
  Joseph 81
  Samuel 31, 42, 81
WOODHULL
  Margaret 25
WOOLSEY
  Miriam 38
WRIGHT
  SEE ALSO ALPHABETICAL
  LISTING IN MAIN TEXT
  Abel 151
  Abraham B 152
  Abraham D 152
  Ambrose 151
  Amelia 152
  Anannias 154
  Anderson 152
  Anthony 54
  Augustus 154
  Belden 152
  Benjamin 151, 154
  Charles C 152
  Christopher 151
  Daniel 32
  David 153
  Ebenezer 153
  Edmund 107
  Elijah 152
  Eliphal 30
  Eliza 152
  Elizabeth 151, 152
  Enos 152
  George 151, 152
  Harriet M 151
  Helen L 152
  Horation N 151, 152
  Isaac R 152, 153
  Jacob 153
  James 151
  James H 152
  James J 153
  John 153, 154
  John F 151
  John H 152
  Jonathan 152
  Joseph 151, 152, 153
  Joshua 54
  Margaret 151
  Mary Elizabeth 154
  Matilda 154
  Nathaniel 153
  Oliver 151
  Olney F 151
  Oscar F 151
  Peter D 151, 152
  Rachel 152
  Robert 152
  Rose 92
  Samuel 153
  Sarah 151
  Silas 151
  Solon 152

WRIGHT cont.
  Susan 154
  Sylvia 152
  Thomas 152, 153
  Temperance 151
  William 151, 153
  William H 153
  William M 153
  Wiltsie A 153
YEOMANS
  Phebe 69
YOUNG
  Naomi 130

www.ingramcontent.com/pod-product-compliance
Lightning Source LLC
Chambersburg PA
CBHW071425160426
43195CB00013B/1807